John Junor's Current Events Column in the *Sunday Express* is probably the most imitated column in British journalism.

Yet it is completely inimitable.

His convictions have the ring of honest coin, his observations the cutting edge of a scalpel, his feelings the refreshing spontaneity of spring water. He is often accused of being acerbic, even savage.

But he can be movingly tender, too, over life's tragedies and triumphs. And always – perhaps above all – humorous, with a wickedly sharp eye for the absurd. It is the best of John Junor.

The best of **JJ**

JOHN JUNOR

Illustrations by Bill Martin

London
UNWIN PAPERBACKS
Boston   Sydney

First published in Great Britain by Sidgwick and Jackson Limited 1981
First published by Unwin Paperbacks 1984

UNWIN ® PAPERBACKS
40 Museum Street, London WC1A 1LU, UK

Unwin Paperbacks
Park Lane, Hemel Hempstead, Herts HP2 4TE, UK

George Allen & Unwin Australia Pty Ltd
8 Napier Street, North Sydney, NSW 2060, Australia

ISBN 0 04 827074 1

Reproduced, printed and bound in Great Britain by
Hazell Watson & Viney Limited,
Member of the BPCC Group,
Aylesbury, Bucks

FOR
SAM AND RODDY AND ALEX

1O DOWNING STREET

THE PRIME MINISTER

20ᵗʰ March 1977.

My dear John,

Alas I don't write
well and could not possibly do
justice to your book in a Foreword.
I could only say that I was
a regular reader, I loved its direct
incisive style, & its capacity to get
to the heart of the matter. And
perhaps I could add that the things
that 'stuck in your gullet' were

the things that should be never
do!

    I fear that would hardly
do for a P.M. and it wouldn't
do justice to a leading editor.

    We must have a talk
again soon.

          In haste
          Yours ever
          Rosebery

A down-page news item caught my eye last week.

It said that pot-holers in the Mendips, near Wells in Somerset, had heard strange underground noises in an adjoining cave — noises that sounded just like a man dragging himself painfully along and occasionally tapping on the rock.

Yet the cave in question had been sealed by sand and gravel for at least two million years.

What or who could it be? May I suggest that next time the pot-holers hear stumbling footsteps, they emit in Gaelic the magic cry: 'You can come out now, Hamish, the office collection's over.'

1 February 1981

·· ·

For just 20 minutes before she died Mrs Anne Murphy was able to cradle in her arms the baby boy to whom against medical advice, she had given birth.

There are many who will say it was crazy and wrong that Mrs Murphy should have died at all when if only she had agreed to an abortion she could still be alive.

I cannot join them. I am not a Roman Catholic. Nor do I believe that the life of an unborn child should always be placed before the life of the mother. But, my God, I respect and admire the faith which imbued Mrs Murphy.

Her child will never know his mother, but there is one thing all his life he will know for sure — that she loved him so much that she gladly gave her life for him.

4 November 1979

·· ·

It must have been a terrifying moment when at 25,000 feet the tail cone blew off that DC9.

But isn't it a mercy that at the time there was not a

passenger sitting in the lavatory in that particular part of the aircraft?

He might well have spent a brief puzzled second in mid air between life and eternity wondering if anything he had done had caused the calamity.

23 September 1979

I do not even know his name. He is a man in a cloth cap I sometimes stand next to in a bus queue.

But that morning he was clearly excited, and wanted to talk. He began telling me about the second-hand caravan he had bought; how he had paid £300 for it; how he had parked it in his garden; how he was going to use it to take his wife and thirteen-year-old daughter on holiday.

His daughter would love that, he said. She had been born with a heart condition. She had spent most of her little life in and out of hospital. Even now she could only sleep propped up on pillows.

That was months ago. Last week I met him again. This time I initiated the conversation. How was the caravan? The caravan, he explained, did not matter any more. His daughter, his only child, had died just before they were due to go on holiday.

There are times when one thanks God for one's own good luck. There are also times when one is humbled beyond measure by the courage with which other people face up to personal and total disaster.

2 October 1977

Explaining that he did not want to send anyone so stupid to jail, a judge in St Albans Crown Court last Friday gave a suspended sentence to an Irishman who had broken into a

shop and stolen microwave ovens in the fond belief that they were television sets.

Isn't it a mercy they caught the poor devil before he cooked himself to a cinder trying to get BBC 2?

22 March 1981

I have seen with my own eyes the affection and respect which existed between Mrs Margaret Thatcher and her official driver, Mr George Newell.

She treated him in the same way as she treats everyone else – as an equal.

George Newell died nine days ago.

His funeral came in a week that has to have been one of the toughest Mrs Thatcher has ever had – a week in which not only Mr Michael Foot but some members of her own Cabinet seem to have been doing their damnedest to destroy her.

In these circumstances it would have been understandable if she had sent a secretary to represent her at the service.

But that is not her style. Last Friday, the Prime Minister was sitting in a pew comforting the widow.

And instead of seeking publicity for her action, Downing Street have done their best to keep the whole matter secret.

I tell you this. The more I see this lady, the more I like her.

15 March 1981

On the wall of his barber's shop in the village of Talana in Sardinia Signor Mario Tegas had a calendar containing a photograph of a nude woman.

Because of that one picture and despite the fact that the barber has since taken it down, the local priest has, for 7 months, refused permission for Signor Tegas to act as godfather at the baptism of his best friend's son.

Now the intercession of the Pope is sought.

Fascinating, isn't it? But the most fascinating thing of all is the reason the local priest gives for his obduracy.

He says: 'Remember there are people here who for months see nothing but goats.'

I don't know how the Pope will react to that argument. But I can tell you it will get sympathetic nods of approval from the elders of the kirk in Auchtermuchty.

23 December 1979

There is every chance that because of a goal scored by Alan Sunderland, in a vital match against Liverpool, Arsenal Football Club will be playing in a money-making tournament in Europe next season.

There is a good deal of evidence which suggested that the

goal should never have been allowed: that it was scored by Mr Sunderland's hand and not his head.

Mr Sunderland refuses to tell us which part of his anatomy put the ball into the net. He says simply: 'I am saying nothing.'

From which taciturnity we may all draw our own conclusions.

I don't suppose it matters a damn. I just feel sad that a great club like Arsenal should be associated with cheating.

5 April 1981

Although it is, alas, outside the realm of my own experience, I expect I might have been momentarily taken aback if Miss Janet Lawler had walked into my office holding her skirt about her head and saying: 'You haven't seen my knickers today, have you?'

Or if at the end of a talk she lifted her pink blouse to her shoulders and said: 'Meeting closed.'

And I sympathize with the embarrassment of Miss Lawler's boss when she took off her sweater, donned a T-shirt and asked him: 'Patrick, can you see my nipples through this?'

These are circumstances in which I would not wish to pre-empt the decision of the Industrial Tribunal as to whether she was unfairly sacked.

But if I were Miss Lawler, and no matter the verdict, I would not feel too downcast. She should remember that for every door that closes, another one opens. And after all the publicity, is there not going to be a queue 3 miles long for her services?

Like to guess which kilted laddies from which town in Scotland are going to be at the head of it?

23 March 1980

Even now I cannot believe that old Gravel Voice is quitting the Prime Ministership.

I feel a real, personal sadness too. For although I detested his politics I liked the man. I have never for one second doubted his compassion for the weak and the suffering. Nor his patriotism. Nor the high quality of his intellect. All I ever doubted was whether between his back stud and his backside there was anything but his braces.

21 March 1976

Duncan Goodhew was just fifteen when his father died.

But when Duncan received his Olympic Gold Medal last Tuesday night, it was his father's old battered flat cap that was on his head.

It was Goodhew's way of paying tribute to a man of whom he later said: 'I felt he was by my side as I swam.'

It says, of course, a good deal for Duncan Goodhew that he should remember a parent with such love.

But does it not say even more for the man, long since dead, who inspired such affection?

27 July 1980

I do not expect Captain Mark Phillips to go around with a halo over his riding cap.

Everyone has a right, on occasion, to lose his or her temper. And a stubborn, struggling horse could test anyone's patience.

But may I offer Captain Phillips some advice?

Should he not wait next time until he is out of range of the cameras and inside the horse box before he plants his size 10 boot into a horse's ribs?

After all, he surely would not want to convey the

impression that given similar provocation he might do exactly the same thing to one of his mother-in-law's corgis.

16 March 1980

••➤••

Next Saturday a sad little procession of elderly members of the War Widows' Association will place a tiny cross of white carnations on the Cenotaph in memory of husbands who died so long ago.

Shortly afterwards the cross, along with all other non-official wreaths, will be removed as the Cenotaph is prepared for the next day's ceremony.

Could not that one cross be allowed to stay?

No. The widows have been told no exception can be made, even for them.

Could not then the widows be represented at the actual Remembrance Day Service? No. They have been told the service is for Government officials and national representatives only.

Funny old country isn't it, when among all the bowed heads in front of the Cenotaph next Sunday the only people missing will be just about the only people who still really care and still really suffer?

5 November 1978

••➤••

With scores of newspaper photographers, TV cameramen, and dirty old men with binoculars in attendance, isn't it marvellous that when Brighton opened its nudist beach only four people took the plunge and that the most photogenic of these should have been a sixty-one-year-old plumber and a fifty-seven-year-old dentist?

Still what else could the Peeping Toms have expected on a chilly blustery April day?

Raquel Welch, Anna Ford, and the president and vice-president of the Auchtermuchty Ladies Curling Club?

6 April 1980

For me the saddest words of the week came from the mother of the little bone-marrow boy, Anthony Nolan.

'My son,' she said, 'is losing the will to live. He just wants to sit on my knee without speaking and have me sing to him. Sometimes he just asks me to go away which he has never done before.'

She described how she had brought Anthony a new toy which she hoped might capture his attention. He looked at it listlessly and did not even try to pick it up.

Poor little Anthony. On Friday he was six.

I hope that the prayers of the world produce a miracle and that he will still be with us at the age of seven.

But if these prayers fail perhaps then we should start

praying for the day when governments the world over will spend less money on things that do not matter, like winning votes, and a good deal more on saving the lives of little children.

4 December 1977

If what he says is true, it must have been deeply disturbing for Mormon missionary Kirk Anderson, kidnapped and shackled to a double bed in a cottage in Devon, to have had his pyjamas ripped off while twenty-seven-year-old former beauty queen Joyce McKinney had her lustful way with him.

Not once, not twice, but thrice.

Poor chap. I sigh for him. But although I have no idea whether she is innocent or guilty and pass no judgment, I must admit that I sigh just a little for Miss McKinney, too.

Perhaps when she is free to do so, she ought to head for Auchtermuchty where not once in the history of that Royal Burgh has there ever been a case of a laddie who has had to be chained and shackled before he would agree to accommodate a lassie.

27 November 1977

The son of Jewish immigrants, Manny Shinwell, was brought up in poverty in the East End of London at a time when the destitute had to scavenge the dustbins for food.

As a boy if he had a farthing to spend he felt rich beyond measure. He had almost no schooling of any kind. At the age of eight, when poverty temporarily prevented his parents maintaining a home together, he was separated from his mother and despatched by rail with a label round his neck to live with his father wherever his father could find work. He became an ardent Socialist and served a prison sentence for his views.

Last week, Manny, now aged ninety-six attended a Press

party to launch his new book *Lead With The Left* – a warm compassionate story which I urge you to buy.

One man who took the trouble to attend was former Tory Prime Minister Lord Home. That fact in itself is an indication of the esteem in which Manny is held. And rightly.

Even at his advanced age, he would still punch in the nose anyone who spoke ill of Britain.

Isn't it extraordinary that he who started with so little should have been so true, while others who started with so much should have so consistently betrayed us?

29 March 1981

··—··

When the Pope arrived in Warsaw, the first thing he did on leaving the plane was to kiss his native Polish soil.

It was an enormously moving moment.

When he went to Ireland, again the first thing he did on leaving the aircraft was to kiss the ground. That puzzled me slightly.

But I was quite mystified when His Holiness also kissed the ground on his arrival in the US.

What can it be all about? Could it be that the Holy Father shares my view about air travel and that when he kisses the ground he is simply saying: 'Thank God I'm safely off that bloody aeroplane'?

14 October 1979

··—··

Did the late Hugh Gaitskell, on a visit to Russia in 1959, drink nineteen tumblers of vodka and then cap that little lot with a tumbler of brandy? Did he, as a result, have to be carried to his car by Denis Healey and David Ennals?

Were there occasions during the war when Winston Churchill was 'paralytically drunk'?

I do not know. Nor do I even care.

What I do know is that drunk or sober both men were immeasurably greater than the third-rate pipsqueak, Lord Avebury, who spits at their memory in safety because they are dead. And does not have the guts to attack anyone who is still alive.

There are people who would have followed Winston Churchill to the ends of the earth.

I would not want even to be in the same room as Lord Avebury without my fingers tightly clenched to my nose.

12 April 1981

••◄►••

The authorities in Atlanta, Georgia, presumably invited Mr Ronald Gregory, Chief Constable of West Yorkshire, to advise them in the hunt for the maniac who has murdered twenty-seven black children because they consider him to be one of our top policemen.

Really? After the 5 years of cock-ups in the hunt for the Yorkshire Ripper?

I wonder whom they would have invited if they had been looking for Britain's best ballet dancer.

Cyril Smith?

17 May 1981

••◄►••

There is all the sadness in the world in the story of Mr Norman Hull who, when he died at the age of seventy-six, left £15 a week to his dog and nothing to his seventy-five-year-old widow.

The dog did not live long to enjoy his 15 quids' worth a week of Pedigree Chum.

Within days of his master's death the widow, on the grounds that the dog was vicious, had him put down.

Me? I take no sides in this human tragedy.

Except to reflect that it must be a pretty grim end to a

marriage, which presumably started so many years ago with high hopes and much love, when a wife feels that her husband cares more for his dog than for her. And, in turn, the husband feels that the only thing that cares a damn for him in life is his poodle.

I feel sympathy for neither of them. But doesn't your heart go out to that poor old pooch?

8 July 1979

‖━‖

Having listened to Mr Roddy Llewellyn burble away aimlessly and vacantly on TV the other night, at least I can now understand why he and Princess Margaret spend their evenings together singing duets such as 'The bells are ringing for me and my gal'.

It must make a welcome rest from the only other activity for which Master Llewellyn would appear intellectually capable.

And just in case any of you read me wrongly, I do mean Noughts and Crosses.

19 February 1978

‖━‖

I knew that winter was ended and the sunshine and warmth were on their way last week when after months of freezing travel on my Waterloo/Dorking service British Rail at last turned on the carriage heat. Full blast.

Lovely people, aren't they, train drivers? *12 April 1981*

‖━‖

The Census form which we are all completing this weekend will tell the Government how many of us have flush toilets, how many of us own or are buying our homes, how many of us are divorced or living in sin, how many cars we have, how we travel to work.

But on one vital issue the census will not provide any information at all – the number of coloured immigrants and their descendants who now live in Britain.

In the 1971 Census some clue was afforded by a question which asked each citizen to state where his or her parents were born.

Now because our coloured population regard it as racialistic even that question has had to be dropped.

Do you suppose they will take a more relaxed view when it is they, not we, who are the majority and their leaders want to find out just how many white ghettos remain in towns like Bradford, Wolverhampton, Leicester, London and Birmingham?

5 April 1981

━━●━━

The eyes of the landlady of the Oliver Cromwell pub in Nechells, Birmingham, must have popped out of her head when she saw at the 'wedding' reception, which the Reverend Arthur Bridge, curate of St Saviour's Church, had helped to arrange, that although the bride wore a blonde wig and a cream-coloured dress, both she and the bridegroom had five o'clock stubble.

And that the bridesmaids had size 11 boots under their frilly frocks.

It cannot have done her digestion much good either to note that when the music started up, the curate joined in the jigging.

The Reverend Mr Bridge's superior, the Bishop of Birmingham, the Right Reverend Hugh Montefiore, said at first that he did not wish to discuss the matter. He has since suspended the curate.

Want to bet that he will not stay long suspended?

Want to bet further that if the Church of England

continues gaily along on its present permissive course the day will not be far distant when at queer wedding receptions the person who dances cheek to cheek with the best man will not be the curate, but the bishop?

22 March 1981

In his 12 years as Editor of the *Sun*, Larry Lamb took its circulation from 650,000 to nearly 4,000,000.

In the process, he made Rupert Murdoch a rich man – rich enough to take over *The Times* and its left-wing sidekick *The Sunday Times*.

Last Monday evening Larry was tossed out on his ear.

In the *Sun* on Tuesday morning I searched in vain for one line about his removal.

In *The Times*, that so-called paper of record, there were just seven.

I would have thought better of Mr Murdoch if he had allowed the editor of his new toy *The Times* and acting editor of his old toy the *Sun* to pay a public tribute to a man who is a greater journalist than all three of them put together.

19 April 1981

⸻

It must have been fascinating, the Press Conference given by the President of Eire, Dr Patrick Hillery.

He summons editors of the main Irish newspapers, representatives of the Irish Broadcasting Company and TV and solemnly tells them that there is no truth in the rumours connecting him with another woman, that his marriage is happy and that he has no intention of resigning as President.

In the middle of the conference he has a telephone conversation with his fifty-year-old wife, Maeve, who is on holiday in Spain. She apparently confirms everything the President has said.

It is an extraordinary tale. But one thing puzzles me. If the rumours were untrue, why bother to deny them?

And even if they were true, is Ireland really a place where a man has to quit public life if he commits adultery?

If so, I applaud the high standards of Irish morality. I also reflect that it is a mercy that the same standards do not apply here.

For if they did, how in God's name could any British Prime Minister of any party ever be able to form a Cabinet?

7 October 1979

⸻

I understand and even agree with the edict making it an offence to sell pheasant and other game during the close season – from 1 February to 30 September.

But isn't it almost unbelievable that, according to the

National Federation of Fishmongers' Newsletter, the same regulation should make it illegal for the shops to sell even tinned game during that same period?

Tinned game? Game tinned maybe 10 years ago and not even shot in Britain?

Do you wonder why I found Mr Harman, my splendid local fishmonger, banging his hapless head against a tray of frozen cod?

19 March 1978

Pope John Paul puts his strong Polish arms around Mrs Kay Kelly and kisses her gently on the forehead.

The comfort he gives Mrs Kelly, who has terminal cancer, is evident in her shining eyes. 'I am in God's hands now,' she says, 'and He will decide the time I die.'

Mrs Kelly said with warmth of the Pope: 'He is a very ordinary person.'

In that she was wrong. The more I see and hear of Pope John Paul the more I am convinced that he is a very extraordinary person indeed.

In an ever darkening world he holds aloft almost the only lamp left.

18 March 1979

The Chinese, we have been led to believe, are just about the most moral race in the world. There is said to be no prostitution. No promiscuity. And outside of marriage no sex.

Is it not, then, extraordinary that the number of black rhinos in Africa has been reduced by 90 per cent in the past 5 years largely because of a great Chinese demand for rhino horn – a product widely believed to have aphrodisiac properties?

What on earth can they be using it for?

Truly, as has been said, only for medicine?

If so, it must be a rum old country where the only time a Chinese lassie's eyes light up is when a Chinese laddie reaches for the cough mixture.

Thank God, it's not like that in Auchtermuchty.

30 September 1979

Black Cuban Lieutenant Colonel Arnaldo Tamayo Mendez, on his orbits of the earth in a Russian spacecraft, took with him photographs of Marx, Engels, Lenin, Che Guevara, Castro, Brezhnev, and Yuri Gagarin, a Cuban flag, a copy of the Cuban National Anthem, samples of sand from the Bay of Pigs, seeds typical of Cuban vegetation, sugar cane, a map of Cuba, a Havana cigar, two poems, a painting, a cartoon, a gold coin, and a bunch of postage

stamps as well as a collection of flags, among them that of the Communist Party of Cuba.

Wouldn't it have been terrible if having remembered to take all that lot with him he had forgotten to take something really vital?

Like his sandwiches?

26 September 1980

""⥤""

Fantastic that a respected forty-five-year-old school secretary from Cheam in Surrey should have spent his spare time climbing bus stop posts and taking away the signs – 965 in all in just 13 months.

Where do you suppose he hid them when he got them home?

Under the bed?

Ah, well! I suppose it takes all sorts to make a world.

But I can tell you this. It would never had happened in Auchtermuchty.

I will not deny that there under a school secretary's bed you might well stub your toe on something which gives a dull clink. But you can be damned sure it is never likely to be a bus stop sign.

21 May 1978

""⥤""

There can be few of us who did not pray for that tiny scrap of humanity, Louise Ann Karen Jane Brown, lying in her cot in a Cardiff hospital.

Just 4 pounds $5\frac{1}{2}$ ounces in weight. One month premature. A baby who will never ever know the mother from whose dead body she was born.

I join in the salute to the twenty-five-year-old doctor, Jane Steiner, who had the skill and the quickness of mind to perform the operation that saved the child.

I don't imagine for one second that there will be any

official honour for Dr Steiner. Such things are reserved for really important people – like hospital administrators.

But then does she need one? For hasn't she the greatest honour of all – an honour that will stay with her for ever: the knowledge that out of death and disaster she has produced life and love?

1 October 1978

I can understand why Prince Charles beat the ground in frustration after he had fallen off Good Prospect last week.

And the anguish with which he said: 'Now I've got to go back and face them all again.'

He must have desperately wanted to win and will be even more determined to keep on trying till he does. He so hates to be seen as a failure.

But is it worth it?

Prince Charles is good at so many things. Would it not

be a mark of greatness rather than of weakness to admit that there is at least one sport in which he is not going to excel?

22 March 1981

Nine-year-old Kirk Peters was born with spina bifida, has a missing lung, a heart murmur, and a weak spine supported by a brace.

He has spent a good deal of his little life in hospital where he is even now recovering from an operation designed to turn an index finger into a thumb.

Yet this little boy, from his hospital bed, writes to PC Stephen Hickling, maimed by the booby-trap bomb in Catford: 'Don't be too sad . . . you can still do loads of things with one hand and I hope you get better very soon.'

Am I the only one to feel humbled by a shining-eyed child who, with so little going for him, has so much courage and so much faith?

25 May 1980

The scene was a tea-room in Pitlochry, with the rain stotting off the pavements outside. I entered into conversation with a grizzled Scot at the adjoining table. He had no idea who I was. But a chance remark of his indicated that he had been a life-long reader of the *Sunday Express*.

Casually, I asked him what he liked best in the paper.

He did not hesitate. 'I always turn first to the John Gordon column.'

Slightly miffed, I pointed out to him that John Gordon has been dead for 2 years.

'Och, aye,' was his reply, 'but it's still the same. Only no so good.'

Wonderful, isn't it, to be famous in Pitlochry?

20 February 1977

No one knew the name of the old man in his eighties who, carrying a battered biscuit tin, walked into Dr Barnardo's home at Barkingside, Ilford. He refused to say who he was.

But it was clear from his dress that he was not a wealthy man.

The tin contained £800 in neatly packaged notes.

Who was he? He is believed to be an ex-Barnardo boy who remembered with gratitude the way that the organization cared for him when no one else would and had spent a lifetime saving up for this final gift.

Whoever he is, I salute him. He is more worthy of praise than half a dozen millionaire philanthropists put together.

1 August 1976

·▬·

When poor old Nelson Rockefeller told his wife on the last night of his life that he would have to work late at the office, he could not have envisaged the furore he was going to leave behind him.

Will the revelations about the precise circumstances in which he died in the company of a lusty lass forty-five years his junior have any lasting effect on his reputation?

You bet they will. In much the same way as the reputation of a President of France Monsieur Felix Faure was affected. Advantageously.

Would anyone today even remember the name of Monsieur Faure had it not been for the fact that when 80 years ago they came to lay out his body after the sudden cerebral haemorrhage he suffered in the Elysée Palace, they first of all had to smuggle out of the back door the young blonde he had been entertaining?

A terrible way to achieve immortality? Maybe.

But isn't it as least a better way to go than dropping off the perch watching *Coronation Street*?

18 February 1979

29

Mrs Eileen Harman awaits the call to become Britain's first heart transplant patient for 5 years.

She is fifty-seven. She knows what the odds against survival are. But she desperately wants to live long enough to see her first grandchild.

And she is brave beyond measure.

She says: 'I know I'll be all right, God determines when I am going to die. Not doctors. If He wanted to take me He could do so just as easily from my bed at home. So I'm ready for the operation as soon as a suitable donor can be found. My bag is packed.'

Don't faith and courage of that order make you feel truly humble?

15 October 1978

•••━••

The Ministry of Agriculture sternly decrees that because he has a testicle one quarter inch shorter than the other, Foxy, a five-year-old Palomino Welsh cob stallion, will have to be gelded.

His owner Mr Alfred Cole faces a £3-a-day fine as long as Foxy stays a stallion.

Isn't that a bit harsh? Why should Foxy, who has sired only two foals anyway, be deprived of his rare moments of ecstasy?

Besides, what does it matter to anyone if a few Palomino Welsh cobs turn out in future to be a little less than perfect?

And how would the civil servants concerned like it if the same cruel criteria were applied to them as they apply to Foxy?

Even though it could be argued that the result would be the finest Civil Service all-male choir the Albert Hall has ever heard.

Soprano, of course.

3 December 1978

Never ever can there have been on television quite as lovely a lady as Commissioner Catherine Bramwell-Booth of the Salvation Army, and grand-daughter of its founder General William Booth.

Wasn't she super? Wasn't her love of life, her gaiety, her vitality at the age of ninety-three joyous and uplifting?

And was not her absolute faith in God touching and beyond measure?

Her grandfather was a bit beyond even my time. But I would like to think that I could impart to my grandchildren just one tenth of the shining faith that he left to his.

10 July 1977

There are occasions when just one unpremeditated act can illustrate far more than words the character of a politician.

It was the first big luncheon party at Chequers immediately after the Election.

At the table were some of the most important people in

the land. The girls serving the meal — they all come from one of the Women's Services — were a little nervous.

The joint, served on a silver salver, had already been carved. As one guest, Mrs William Whitelaw, helped herself to a slice of the joint, the girl carrying the salver inclined it just a little too much towards Mrs Whitelaw's plate.

Suddenly there was disaster. The joint slipped off the salver and, en route to the floor, much of the gravy and some of the lamb ended up over the collar and suit of the Chancellor, Sir Geoffrey Howe.

There was stunned silence. Then the Prime Minister was on her feet, running to the other side of the table. Not to console Sir Geoffrey Howe but to put her arms around the serving girl, and to say to her: 'Don't worry, my dear. Don't worry. It could happen to anyone.'

I tell you again. The more I hear and see of Mrs Thatcher the more I like her.

4 November 1979

··➤··

For 33 years, Mrs Evelyne Green refused to accept that her only child, an airgunner shot down over Germany, was dead.

She kept his room as it had been. His books, his model airplane exactly as he had left them.

And when she died, she left her entire fortune to him and stipulated that the search for him be continued.

There are some will say she was crazy. I am not among them.

For despite her wealth, probably the only thing she had to hold on to in life was the forlorn hope that she might one day see her son again.

Is it not better to live in hope, however far-fetched, than with no hope at all?

24 October 1976

There was near panic when two twenty-one-year-old Scottish athletes at the Commonwealth Games in Edmonton were found to be missing from their own beds at 2 a.m.

And uproar when it was discovered that they were in the girls' section.

Where on earth did they expect two normal Scottish laddies missing from their own beds, and after the bars were closed, to be?

Looking for fairies at the bottom of the garden?

6 August 1978

From a long forgotten war of 100 years ago a sad little story emerged in Sotheby's sale room.

The Victoria Cross won in 1880 by Gunner James Collis, Royal Horse Artillery, for 'conspicuous bravery' during a retreat in the Afghan War fetched £5,800.

We now learn that because he subsequently committed bigamy Gunner Collis was stripped of his VC.

Poor Gunner Collis, long, long dead.

Wasn't it unjust that he should have been so harshly treated?

I would like to think that God has dealt with him more kindly.

And given the only thing possible to a man brave enough to take on two wives at the same time.

A heavenly bar to his VC.

25 March 1979

Lesley-Anne Down has been telling how she came to make her sudden decision to jilt the man she had lived with for

10 years, and to marry an unknown Argentinian film assistant 4 years younger than herself.

'It's like sometimes you fancy egg and chips,' she says, 'other times you fancy steak and tomatoes. I fancied Ricky. He is Latin, passionate – what more do you want? Besides which the local vodka in Budapest is very strong you know.'

Yes indeed, I do know. But if it is hot, tempestuous passion she seeks, and alcohol that turns her on, isn't it a mercy that she was filming in Hungary and not in Scotland?

Three slugs of the Grand McNish in the Hollies and she could well have ended up in bed with half the members of the Auchtermuchty Curling Club.

6 March 1981

<hr style="width: 10%">

Roy Harthill, aged twenty-five, roped his six-year-old son, a frail little boy with a hole in the heart, to a bed and beat him with a belt.

When his wife complained he told her that the sooner the boy was in his wooden box the better.

And after all that, Roy Harthill walked out of court a free man on a suspended sentence.

It was said in his defence that the child still shows great affection for his father. And that I believe. The humbling wonderful thing about children is that like puppies they still show pathetic love even for the cruel men to whom they feel they belong.

I hope that the court was wiser than courts sometimes are. But my Christmas thoughts and prayers are with that little six-year-old child.

18 December 1977

I do not suppose we will ever know for sure just why escaped prisoner George Wicks, after 10 years of freedom and having served only 9 months of a 7-year sentence, should knock on the door of Wormwood Scrubs and plaintively ask: 'Please may I come back in?'

But I would suspect that it has to be a woman who triggered it off.

Desperate old world isn't it, when a man would rather spend another 7 years in jail than another 10 minutes of his loved one's tongue?

20 July 1980

The story of that baby gorilla, Toto, just ten-weeks-old, just 5 pounds in weight and blubbering pathetically as she is put back in her packing-case and sent on to Japan, is going to stay in my mind for a long time.

We are told that there was nothing illegal about her departure from her native Cameroon and that her sale for money was lawful, even though baby gorillas, just like human children, are utterly dependent on their mothers for the first 3 years of their lives.

For my own part, I think the whole lousy business of trafficking in wild animals stinks.

The Good Book says that not a sparrow falls, not even when shot down in church by an English vicar, without God being aware. Might that not also apply to a baby gorilla crying pathetically for her mother?

9 September 1979

It is a matter of chance that I did not begin the week in the obituary columns.

On my way home late last Saturday night the offside rear wheel fell off my car.

Luckily, on a fast bend on a wet country road 24 miles

from London, I sensed that something was terribly wrong. I was at a standstill when the wheel fell off.

Examination showed that the nuts on the other rear wheel were not even finger-tight.

The car had been delivered only that afternoon after a major service in which the two rear wheels had been taken off.

The mechanic who did the service swears that the nuts were properly tightened. There is no possible way in which I could challenge his honesty.

But what alternative remains?

Please God may it not be that either Wedgwood Benn or the jealous husband of a member of the Auchtermuchty Women's Institute has finally gone completely bananas.

8 June 1980

∎━∎

There were moments last week when I did not give a damn what happened at the Arab – Israeli talks nor even about the £520 million a year which British Steel is losing.

As the ice formed inches thick on my water-butt, and the snow lay deep on the ground, I was thinking of eight-year-old Lester Chapman on his own and without food or proper shelter.

Of a nipper of eight who writes a letter to his mother and stepfather, who apparently wanted him taken into care: 'Please don't come and find me. I can look after myself.'

I would like to think, if he is still alive – and please God may he be – that that little boy for the rest of his life will know that he is loved and wanted.

22 January 1978

∎━∎

PC Stanley Thomas must have had difficulty in keeping a straight face when he told a court in Morecambe, Lancashire, of his arrival in a village where a lioness cub had escaped and of the predicament in which he found a colleague, Lancashire's biggest policeman, 6 feet 10 inches tall, 16-stone PC Adrian Myhill.

Said PC Thomas: 'When I arrived on the scene, I saw PC Myhill running across a field closely followed by a lioness and an Alsatian dog.'

Every time I read that sentence I collapse in helpless laughter.

Am I taking the mickey out of PC Adrian Myhill? In no way.

I tell him this. If I had been in the same field with him and pursued by the same lioness and Alsatian, I would have been half a yard ahead of him.

30 April 1978

When thirty-three-year-old Mike McMullen left Plymouth on 5 June on the single-handed Transatlantic race, there were some who no doubt wondered how he could bring himself to do so when only 4 days previously his wife had died – electrocuted while helping him with the final preparations on his boat.

But sometimes it is not only those who weep the most who mourn the most.

Now it appears that Mike McMullen – long overdue – may be dead too. If that, unhappily, should be so, there are those who will argue that in his state of mind he should never have been allowed to leave Plymouth. I am not among them.

He did what he felt he had to do. And I suspect he was the sort of person who would rather be lost at sea with the bitter-sweet memory of a lost love in his heart at the age of thirty-three than be pushed around in a wheelchair at the age of eighty.

18 July 1976

On my holiday in Normandy I was bitten in the leg by a French bitch – of the four-legged variety alas.

Within minutes I was in the village doctor's surgery.

No queues. No receptionists.

Just welcomed by the doctor himself. The wound cleaned and bandaged. An injection given against tetanus.

Five minutes later and 38 francs (£4.50) the poorer, I was out on the street reflecting that the French medical service, which deters people with trivial complaints by charging the patient the full price at the time then reimbursing 90 per cent of it later, has a lot to be said for it.

And how is the bite?

My friends on the Press Council and elsewhere may be

disappointed to learn that so far there are no signs of rabies. The bitch was less fortunate. It was 6 days before she stopped being sick.

3 September 1978

There were no Press photographers' bulbs flashing when Sir Max Aitken left the Express building for the last time as Chairman of Beaverbrook Newspapers.

Why should there be? Who the hell cares about an old king when there is a new emperor?

I do.

Max Aitken, DSO, DFC, Battle of Britain night fighter pilot at a time when, with his power and influence, he could have been sitting at a snug desk, is not only one of the bravest men I have ever known. He was also the best boss and the best friend anyone could ever hope for.

3 July 1977

Years ago when they set the lions free to roam at Whipsnade Zoo, it is said that the lions long afterwards continued to pace up and down where once the bars had been.

Now I hear that in Cardiff where they have turned the city centre into a traffic-free shopping precinct, the citizens still religiously cross the road only where the pedestrian crossing used to be.

Funny creatures lions. Splendid people the Welsh.

23 November 1975

Can you imagine the anguish of the mother of six-year-old leukemia victim Jamie MacColl when, as they passed a grave being dug in a cemetery, the little boy clutched her hand

and asked her: 'Mummy I'm too young to die, aren't I?'

At that time, most children who contracted the disease died within weeks.

But that was 3 years ago. And Jamie is not only still alive, but fit and tough and well.

Blessed indeed are the men and women who have fought to save him, the dedicated researchers and hospital doctors who have brought hope to children like Jamie where once there was none.

There are times when I feel they are worth more than all our politicians stuffed together.

11 July 1976

It must have been disconcerting for the Kimono-clad stewardess on the Japanese jumbo who, when she went to answer a bell pressed by a passenger in the aircraft's top deck sleeper section, discovered that the bell had not been pushed deliberately by his finger but accidentally by another part of his anatomy as he turned to get a better manoeuvring position in a bed designed for one but in fact occupied by two.

Equally the male steward who answered a summons and found a naked middle-aged lady asking him to massage her back must have been slightly put out.

Are you comforted by this evidence that not all Japanese have their minds fixed on increasing export targets?

I would be too were it not for one niggling fact. The nationality of the passengers concerned has not been given. Is it just possible that they were not Japanese at all but members of the Tokyo Caledonian Society on their way back home to Auchtermuchty?

26 November 1978

Little Frank was just fourteen years old when he came home one night from a visit to a youth club in Torquay to find that his father, mother and two younger brothers had disappeared.

So, too, had all the furniture, apart from a bed and a wardrobe.

Frank had been deserted.

For almost 2 years he lived like a stray dog, sleeping where he could, begging meals from neighbours, running away from one foster home after another, stealing from time to time, and being caught from time to time.

Eventually he was sent to Borstal. There officials began to try to trace his parents.

When they were found 3 weeks ago, Frank hugged his mother and shook hands with his father.

Do you wonder when you read a pathetic story like this why some children go wrong? And why the probability is that little Frank will go on to much bigger and more tragic headlines?

But what can you do, what can you say about parents who treat their own son in a way you wouldn't treat a mongrel pup?

2 March 1975

There can hardly be a middle-aged woman in the land who did not say 'silly old fool', when it was announced that, at the age of eighty, Fred Astaire was to get married again – to a lady 45 years younger than himself.

Me? I am on Fred's side. He will get the company of a beautiful woman – and one who, I have no doubt, genuinely cares for him.

She will have the honour of having been however briefly, Mrs Astaire.

And if the excitement of sharing a bedroom with a

shapely lass should cause Fred to fall off the perch, so what?

Can you think of a better way of going?

9 March 1980

••◄••

Mr John Lee, Socialist MP for Birmingham Handsworth, believes that lusty ladies are having their wicked way with innocent, defenceless men. He wants the law changed so that such women can be charged with rape.

Is he having us all on? And if not, couldn't he at least give us a hint as to where in England these dreadful crimes are being committed?

Is he unaware that in the neck of the woods from which I hail, there are eager, panting kilted laddies hanging on his words and waiting to catch the next train South?

29 October 1978

••◄••

As I drove home along a lonely road at the height of last week's storm, I saw in my headlights two figures struggling against the ferocious wind and rain. A woman and a child of no more than three.

I hesitated for a second before I stopped.

'Have you far to go?' I cried out.

There was some hesitation too on the woman's part before she and her little sobbing son climbed into the warmth of the car. Her own car, she told me, had skidded off the road. She had already walked one mile with her child in these dreadful conditions. Within a few minutes I had her and the little boy safely at their home.

But as I drove off again I reflected.

Isn't it a bloody society when the traveller has to hesitate before giving help and the person who desperately needs help has to hesitate before accepting it?

15 January 1978

If it is really true, as Italian nutritionists tell us, that if you make love twice a week for a year you will lose 9.13 pounds in flab, then I can tell you one thing for sure.

They are never going to run short of bean-poles in Auchtermuchty.

I was moved by the story of the late Mr Tom Hancock's gold watch.

It was the eighty-seven-year-old man's most treasured possession. Perhaps because it represented the only mark of honour he had ever received. It had been presented to him by his employers to mark 50 years of loyal service in the brickyards.

He kept it tucked away in a safe place and only ever wore it when he went for a reunion dinner with his old workmates.

When he died, and to avoid family squabbles, he insisted in his will that his seven sons should draw lots for it.

Poor old Tom? No marvellous old Tom.

I would just like to think that the son who won the watch will treasure it as much as his old dad did.

30 April 1978

It must have been an exciting moment for the economy-class passengers on a National Airlines plane when out of the first-class section emerged a shapely, naked young blonde waving a champagne bottle and saying: 'I have just inherited five million dollars and am celebrating'.

Why does nothing like that ever happen to me on a journey?

My luck is such that if ever on a night sleeper trip to

Glasgow I heard a tapping on the wall of the next compartment it would almost certainly be a bearded highlander putting his dentures in the tooth mug.

25 June 1978

It is said that in the house of the couple who swopped their baby for a clapped-out £20 Vauxhall Viva car there was no table. Their children's food was set out on the floor and the kids had often to compete for it with the family Alsatian.

Normally children cling instinctively even to the worst of parents. But in this case, the eldest child, a boy, just seven years old, had pleaded with the NSPCC to be taken into care.

Poor little soul. Please God – may the day come when he will be able to give to children of his own the love and protection he has not so far received himself.

22 July 1979

Did you chance to see that wonderful TV programme on the life of Robert Burns?

And if so, did you reflect as I did, that in his 37 bawdy years of wine, women and poetry, Robert Burns, who died not worth a tosser, did more to enrich humanity than all the ministers of religion and all the politicians, and all the business men of his time put together?

29 January 1978

＊＊＊

As someone with an inbuilt suspicion of both ends of a horse, I bow to the superior wisdom of Princess Anne and Prince Philip on all matters equine.

I accept the Princess's assertion that there is no cruelty to horses in making them jump prodigious heights.

I do not argue with Prince Philip when he defends the use of pain-killing drugs and reviving by artificial means of horses exhausted during a competition.

I just utter one little prayer.

Feeling as they do, wouldn't it be wonderful for both of them if in some future life they returned to this earth as show-jumping horses stuffed with phenylbutazone and capable at the flick of a riding crop, preferably held by someone like Harvey Smith, of clearing an 8-foot wall?

7 September 1980

＊＊＊

In a thin cotton shirt and with only 8p in his pocket, twelve-year-old Vincent Kelly arrives shivering in sleet and snow at Leighton Buzzard and asks to see his granny.

I can understand his grandmother's agitation on learning that he had stowed away in an airliner in South Africa and had made his way unaided from Heathrow Airport to Leighton Buzzard.

I can even understand her fear that he might run away again.

But no matter how big a dare-devil he is and how kindly the police treated him, was it really necessary that a boy so obviously and so desperately seeking affection should have to spend his first night in this country in a police cell, the next one in a children's home and then have a close guard of security men, detectives and uniformed police when he was put on the plane taking him home?

Was there no one at all to make a twelve-year-old boy feel that he was loved and wanted?

18 March 1979

◆━◆

That tough hero of the screen, James Garner, seems to be somewhat gentler in real life.

When, after a minor road accident, the other driver lost his cool and hit Mr Garner and kicked him in the head, our screen hero pretended he was unconscious in the hope that the other chap would stop kicking, but he didn't.

What did Mr Garner do then?

'I laid still but got kicked in the head again,' he told a court in Santa Monica.

Didn't he even try to land a blow in self-defence?

'No', said Mr Garner. 'But I did try to bite him.'

Bite him? Bite him with his teeth?

Judged by all the other facts of the case, isn't it a mercy he just happened to have them with him?

22 June 1980

◆━◆

No matter how she appeared on the surface, nine-year-old Zoe Miller must have been scared stiff every time she flew in her father's tiny Auster plane with her mother and her sister.

For she tucked a note in her pocket giving her name and address and saying: 'Please take care of my cat and poodle if anything happens to us.'

Something did happen. The plane crashed. The note was found by the police on Zoe's dead body. They passed it on to a family friend.

That same afternoon the friend took the poodle and the cat to a vet and had them both destroyed.

I pass no judgment on anyone. But doesn't your heart go out to a little girl whose last pathetic wish counted for nothing?

30 May 1976

On my commuter train home from London in the evening, I have long noticed that while the women stay awake and busy themselves with their books, their newspapers, their knitting, or their yapping, most of the men in the carriage, even the young men, are soon fast asleep.

Charitably, I have put it down to the extra stress and strain involved either in their work or in their lunchtime drinking.

But now I remark a new trend. Exactly the same thing is happening in the morning.

Why do you suppose the men are so flaked out that they fall asleep even on their way to work, and the women, in contrast, look so smug and well contented?

Could it possibly be that in my neck of the woods some lassies have been paying not a blind bit of notice to that recent edict of three judges that once a week is ample?

14 December 1980

■■━●■■

At the age of four, financed by the pennies collected from fellow parishioners, Natalie Clamp was taken by her mother to Lourdes in search of a miracle cure for the cystic fibrosis which had afflicted her from the age of four months.

But the miracle was not to be. And little Natalie said: 'Let's go home to Daddy.'

On the flight home, minutes before their plane touched down at Luton, Natalie died in her mother's arms.

Pathetic? Yes. But was it also wrong that the trip to Lourdes should have been made and hope held out for a cure that could never be?

I do not think so. I salute and respect the faith of a mother who flew to Lourdes with hope in her heart. And returned with a dead baby in her arms.

2 May 1976

■■━●■■

If Sir Charles Forte wished to do so he could make a bomb by allowing gambling in his vast chain of Trust House Forte hotels.

But he refuses to do so.

He says: 'I don't believe in gambling. I am not in business to take other people's hard-earned cash for nothing.'

If we had more business men who put principle before profit like Charles Forte and more inspired religious leaders than the dead-beats we now have, then perhaps we would no longer live in a society in which there are bigger crowds in betting shops than there ever are in churches.

12 March 1978

Poet Laureate Cecil Day-Lewis was not only unfaithful to his wife, he was unfaithful to his mistress. And when he had a wife and two mistresses at the same time, he was unfaithful to all three of them, and ran off to marry a woman twenty years younger than himself, leaving his wife and children and mistresses stranded.

And it would appear that he didn't really give a damn for any of them.

For when he lay dying he said to a friend: 'I knew that writing poetry was the point of my life. Everything else took a very secondary place indeed.'

Now 8 years after his death the son whom he walked out on writes his father's biography. A biography full of bitterness and bile? In no way. A biography instead full only of love and understanding.

The poetry for which Cecil Day-Lewis cared so much is now largely forgotten. Yet I would hesitate to call his a wasted life.

Isn't it any man's best memorial to leave behind a son who loved him?

30 March 1980

It must have been quite a moment when thirty sweaty, naked Plymouth rugby players raced into the showers and found there twenty-two naked lady hockey players.

Isn't it marvellous that as feminine screams rent the air, the rugby players acted like true gentlemen, averted their eyes, put towels round their waists and retreated to their changing rooms?

It says a great deal for the English.

I would like to think that my own race would act with equal chivalry. But I have to admit that I can visualize only one circumstance in which the same thing might happen in Auchtermuchty: if the lassies under the showers were

members of the Church Ladies' Guild. And then there would not be a polite retreat. But a panic-stricken stampede.

13 January 1980

What constitutes success in life?

The power and fame one has achieved?

I think not.

When the news of Lady Hailsham's death was gently broken to her four-year-old grandson, the child burst into tears and said: 'She was my bestest friend.'

Could anyone really have a better epitaph?

28 May 1978

＊＊＊＊＊＊

Ironic, isn't it, that Vancouver cyclist John Hatherway should pedal 43,200 miles round the world in 86 weeks without incident, only to have his bicycle nicked when he left it for just 3 minutes outside a shop in Salford?

Still, I suppose he can be thankful it was Salford. In some parts of London, Heathrow Airport for example, in the same 3 minutes he would have lost his belt and braces too.

11 July 1976

＊＊＊＊＊＊

When Jeanne Western died her estate totalled £32,000 — the proceeds of a lifetime of prostitution.

And she left all of it for cancer research.

How should we judge Mrs Western?

As a woman who lived an evil life? Or as a woman who amassed a fortune for the benefit of others?

I offer no opinion.

But when the Day of Judgment comes, who do you reckon will be held to have done the greater good with their lives? A whore like Jeanne Western? Or some of our present trendy clerics in the Church of England?

14 September 1975

In Russia Dr Naum Khodakov has a smash hit best seller with his book advising young Soviet couples on how to make a success of marriage.

What sort of advice does it contain?

One of Dr Khodakov's specimen problems concerns a patient who was worried because he and his wife could obtain full sexual satisfaction only if the husband dressed in woman's underwear and if she called him by a woman's name.

Dr Khodakov's counsel? Stop worrying. Go ahead and enjoy it.

I wonder why the Soviet authorities, who invariably try to convey the impression that everything in Russia is flawless, should admit that such kinkiness even exists.

Could it be that at home some of the grim hatchet-faced members of the Politburo wear frilly panties and answer to the name of Lassie?

28 October 1979

••—••

For the last 19 years the crowds have roared at the skill of England and Chelsea goalkeeper Peter Bonetti. There has been all the heady excitement of London life. The glamour of trips to the capitals of the world.

Now instead of seeking a job in soccer management he retires with his wife and family to run a little hotel on the Hebridean island of Mull where just about the most exciting sound is that of a trout leaping in Loch Ba.

And the most glamourous evening out, a ceilidh in Tobermory with Bobby McLeod playing the accordion, rosy-cheeked lassies singing Gaelic songs and Angus Macin-tyre reciting his poems.

And yet I envy him.

I envy him the soft rain, the mist-covered hills and most of all the warm friendship of people to whom worldly fame means little. He may find there a happiness and a serenity unknown in football's rat-race.

20 May 1979

When nineteen-year-old labourer Mark Hartley had a row with the woman with whom he was living, he went into her ten-year-old daughter's bedroom after midnight and sexually assaulted her while her two little sisters slept alongside.

Hartley had a long record of sexual offences.

Yet magistrates at Coleshill, near Birmingham, allowed him to walk out of the dock a free man with a suspended 6-month sentence.

The child's mother rushed to embrace him – an embrace which suggests that they are together again.

Doesn't anyone on that magistrates' bench give a damn for a ten-year-old child who from now on will lie in bed at night in fear and trembling?

25 March 1979

By most people's standards Robin Day is a celebrity.

He makes a handsome income. He is on Christian name terms with top politicians.

But I wonder how much that counted to Robin Day during the long hours earlier this month as he sat beside his five-year-old son at University College Hospital, holding the child's hand and praying that he might come out of a coma into which his fall of 25 feet on to a concrete pavement had put him?

I rejoice that Robin's little boy, although still in hospital, is making a good recovery.

But does not an accident like this strike home to people

like Robin Day and to all other parents just where real wealth, real happiness, and real success lie?

Look again at the bright-eyed treasures around you this Sunday morning.

25 December 1978

I congratulate Captain Caroline Frost and First Officer Lesley Hardy on being the first all-women crew of a British airliner.

I congratulate also the passengers on the trip from Southend to Dusseldorf who accepted with typical British phlegm the fact that both first officer and captain were ladies.

But my heart goes out to the German business men who, on an earlier trip with Captain Frost, petrified by the thought of a lassie at the controls, stood up and cheered when the plane landed safely.

I have to confess that this cowardy custard is with them all the way.

I will happily accept a woman as Prime Minister; as Chancellor of the Exchequer; even as my bank manager.

But when it comes to flying through ten tenths cloud or in a snow storm, please God give me a pilot who wears a belt and braces and smokes a pipe.

6 November 1977

Mr Spiro Agnew did not have too many friends when in disgrace, destitute, owing $200,000 and facing corruption charges, he was forced to quit as Vice President of the United States.

But he had one.

Frank Sinatra, without asking anything – even a promissory note – in return, made $200,000 available to him so that he could start his life again.

And the only reason we now learn of the incident is because Mr Agnew chooses to tell us.

Frank Sinatra is not my favourite person. But doesn't this shed a new light on his character?

And on Mr Agnew's too?

For can a man be wholly bad who freely acknowledges the debt he owes to another?

18 May 1980

Marvellous little country isn't it, in which an industrial tribunal should not only award £903 compensation to Mr Mohammed Ayub, who was sacked after having been found with his shoes and socks off and hands tucked under his left cheek snugly asleep in bed while on the night shift, but should also recommend that Vauxhall Motors take him back?

Isn't it a mercy that they didn't at the same time put him up for the OBE?

Still, I do not suppose for one second that Mr Ayub is the only sinner around the factory.

A shop steward who gave evidence for him was threatened with lynching by other workers at Luton. It was said in court that Mr Ayub's reinstatement could cause a strike.

Why? Can it really be that production workers at Vauxhall are incensed at the thought of anyone having a quiet zizz on night shift?

If you believe that you will, alas, believe anything. My strong suspicion is that the reason for their anger is not because they have anything against sleeping but because they take the view that such a perk should be reserved only for whites.

Do you really wonder why the Japanese car-workers are falling over themselves laughing on their way to the bank?

23 July 1978

••——••

Moving, the story of how when Andy Kane, fifty-nine, dropped dead in the street his eight-year-old Alsatian would not let anyone near him.

The dog stood guard by his master's body until it, too, lay dead, shot by a policeman's bullet.

I know nothing about Andy Kane. But I tell you this. If he was loved as much by his wife and family as he was by his dog, then he must have been a very happy and a very lucky man.

20 June 1976

••——••

It is, of course, a richly comic situation when a farm hand sees a movement in the long grass, thinks it is a rabbit, lets fly with both barrels and up jumps a man with his trousers round his ankles yelling 'A-a-a-rgh!'

I did not find it so funny. I think the man in question, Mr Dennis Hammerton has had a very rough deal indeed.

Mr Justice Bristow described Mr Hammerton as 'eaten up with spite' against the man who shot him.

I am bound to tell you that if I had been permanently blinded in one eye I would have been feeling pretty sore too.

For is it really now to be accepted as law that a man out shooting rabbits has a right to blaze away at anything moving in the long grass without even having identified what is moving?

And would Mr Justice Bristow have reached the same judgment if it had been not a man making love but an innocent toddler picking buttercups? Or even a High Court judge enjoying a picnic?

23 July 1978

Martha Mitchell was a loud-mouthed lady. But she couldn't always have been like that. There must at some time have existed between her and her husband, ex-United States Attorney-General John Mitchell, love and warmth and affection.

Isn't it sad that love can turn to such hate that she died alone and friendless in a New York hospital?

Her husband knew she was dying. But he stayed away. So did Martha's fifteen-year-old daughter. I can just understand the husband. But for a child to stay away – or be kept away – from her own mother?

A hatred which can go to such bitter lengths is beyond my comprehension.

6 June 1976

The sex manual which China has just issued to two million of its young people advises them that if they wish to break the sex habit, they should: 'avoid all sexually exciting substances such as tobacco and alcohol, shun pornographic films and books and wear baggy underpants.'

The manual also says that: 'if on the morning after having sex a couple feel worn-out, heavy-headed, have pain in the thighs or are short of breath, or if they detect a loss of appetite, they are having too much sex and should take corrective measures.'

What sort of corrective measures, I wonder?

Have they ever thought about turning the baggy underpants back-to-front?

9 November 1980

Mr Malcolm Muggeridge has for so long been a symbol of moral righteousness and of the crusade against permissiveness that it is difficult to envisage a time when a halo of purity did not surround his saintly seventy-seven-year-old head.

Now we learn that for much of his life he has been an active pursuer of beautiful birds. And had torrid affairs with lovely Indian ladies.

His biographer, Mr Ian Hunter, writes: 'From an early age, Muggeridge had sex on his mind . . . for most of his life he has been torn between forswearing lust and yielding to it with a delicious shiver.'

Do these revelations reduce my regard for Mr Muggeridge? Not at all.

I respect the way he has turned his face away from temptation. But isn't it marvellous that wisely he waited to do so until an age so advanced that the only bird still likely to attract him would be the roast turkey on Christmas Day?

9 November 1980

It seems so little to ask, the request which Mr Christ Behiri, a Greek Cypriot waiter at the White Tower Restaurant in Soho, is making.

Mr Behiri, one of the gentlest, kindest men I know, wants permission to take his wife and three children to visit for one hour, just one hour, the father whom he has not seen for 7 years.

If he does not see his father soon he never will. For the old man is ninety years of age.

For 7 years Mr Behiri has saved to make the trip to Cyprus. On 7 August he will set off with his family.

But will he be able to see his father? Will there be tears, and kisses, joy and laughter in the reunion of loved ones? No.

For the father lives in the Turkish controlled part of Cyprus. And the Turkish authorities refuse permission for Mr Behiri to enter the area. Not even for one hour. Not even to say a last goodbye to his father.

These are truly times when I feel that even the beasts of the field must feel ashamed to share the same world as men who can act with such lack of compassion.

16 July 1978

In Blaenau, Gwent, the sound is of harps being plucked and fiddles tuned and glasses polished for the jig of the year.

There Idris Pope has completed nearly 50 years' service as councillor in the Abertillery area. And in that joyous, open-hearted fashion which characterizes the Socialist movement his comrades on the Borough Council are to honour him.

He is to be made the first freeman of the Borough. Good Old Idris.

He is to be presented with a silver casket costing

£750. Wonderful. Won't that look nice on the sitting room mantelpiece?

And afterwards there is to be a dance for 400.

Isn't that marvellous?

And how much are his comrades contributing per head for all this? Not even an old trouser button. The entire tab will be picked up by the ratepayer.

Still, isn't it a mercy to know that with any luck it might even be their own 5p pieces they toss, with gay abandon, into the cloakroom collecting saucer? Provided, of course, they are not claiming £11-a-day attendance money.

6 August 1978

In the sad, strange story of the couple who wanted a baby by artificial insemination and chose a nineteen-year-old prostitute as the mother, there is much cause for anger and distress.

Anger at the unnamed doctor who for thirty dirty pound notes carried out the operation.

Distress at the thought that one day the child may learn the truth.

Yet is it not touching that the couple should have been prepared not only to hand over £3,500, every penny of their life savings, in order to have a child, but also their car and their house?

And isn't it touching too that the young prostitute who had entered into the transaction sordidly for money suddenly discovered when the child was born that it meant more to her than all the money in the world?

Are any of these three in the eyes of God less deserving of mercy than the trendy lady who with the help of a trendy doctor denies the right of an unwanted baby to live at all?

25 June 1978

Funny old world, isn't it, when millions of chickens may be slaughtered because they are producing eggs in such quantities as to make them cheap enough for old age pensioners to eat?

10 September 1978

Woman magazine tells us that the average married woman in England makes love only two and a half times a week.

Only two and a half times a week? Could this explain why the trains from the South are always so jammed full with English ladies heading North to see the wondrous sights of Auchtermuchty?

Although on second thoughts, and since the average must include the many who never make love at all, could it also explain why there are some English lassies who haven't even enough energy left to get to the station?

22 January 1978

It is just 4 years since Mr David Steel and the rest of the Liberal Party were fawning over Mr Jeremy Thorpe as in his tweed suit and green pork-pie hat he helicoptered up and down the country bestowing benedictions on Liberal candidates.

If he had tossed a tulip at Cyril Smith in Rochdale, dear old fat Cyril would have caught it in his teeth and performed a ballet dance in ecstasy.

If he had said a kind word to Mr Steel, Mr Steel would have rolled on his back like a love-sick spaniel.

Now, terrified by the thought that contact with him might cost them their own seats, the Liberals treat Mr

Thorpe as if he'd stopped using deodorant. They even try to ban him from their Conference.

Aren't they a miserable, lousy, cowardly bunch? Don't they even pay lip service to the principle that a man is innocent until he is proved guilty?

10 September 1978

=—=

Whatever Mrs Maureen Colquhoun, that unattractive lady who sits as Labour MP for Northampton North, does after she turns out the light and climbs into bed at night is her own affair.

But couldn't she have kept it that way? Does she really have to pour her heart out to *Women's Own* and say of the woman with whom she now lives: 'I fell in love with Barbara Todd as heavily as I first fell in love with Keith Colquhoun.'

Has she considered what the effects of flaunting her lesbianism might be on her three children?

Does she imagine it helps them very much to have the whole world know that every night their elderly mum chases another elderly and equally unprepossessing lady round the bedroom?

Ugh!

17 September 1978

=—=

Sandy Copland's two little sons, one aged eighteen months, the other two and a half, are buried in a Somerset churchyard.

Mr Copland, a New Zealander, and one of the best farmers in Britain, has lived here since 1942.

Now nearing retirement, he plans to go back home to live. But he means from time to time to return to this country to visit the graves of the two little boys he loved and lost.

Because of this, he would like dual nationality and has applied for a British passport. So that when he does come back he will not have to queue up through the door designed for aliens.

But his request has been turned down.

Funny old world, isn't it, when a man like Sandy Copland may have to ask a Pakistani immigration officer's permission before he is allowed to visit the graves of his own little children?

1 January 1978

＊～＊

Early morning commuters at Huntingdon rubbed their eyes with bewilderment when they clambered aboard the 8.10 to King's Cross on 21 March.

There was not just one buffet car in the train which had started earlier that morning from Leeds. There were two.

There was also a fully operational restaurant car with a chef and a waitress.

On arrival at King's Cross, according to one commuter who wrote to the London *Evening Standard*, there was an army of porters waiting.

What can have happened?

I accept British Rail's explanation that the extra catering facilities were occasioned only by the need to get rolling stock back to London and that it was a mere coincidence that a party of senior British Rail officials just happened to be aboard that train.

Of course, of course.

All I ask is that one day I may suffer a similar coincidence on the 8.26 cattle truck from Horsham to London.

Perhaps it might then be possible between Wimbledon and Waterloo to turn the page of a newspaper without

running the risk of being accused of having made an
improper advance to three different ladies.

1 April 1979

Rum little story, the case of Royal Chaplain the Venerable
John Youens.

The evidence given by two policemen against sixty-
three-year-old Archdeacon Youens was clear and explicit.

They said that a girl aged about fourteen and wearing
long light brown stockings with white tops was standing on
an oil drum outside Wimbledon No. 1 Court watching an
Ilie Nastase match.

They said that with their own eyes they saw the archdeacon lift her skirt exposing her thighs four times.

Yet isn't it extraordinary that when the two policemen
arrested the archdeacon after his fourth lifting of the

lassie's skirt they did not ask the name and address of the lassie herself?

Did she not even complain? Or was she so busy watching Ilie Nastase's backhand that she was unaware of the archdeacon's left hand?

I agree with the decision of the court to acquit the archdeacon.

But what is going to happen to the two police officers concerned?

Are they going to be back in court tomorrow or next week, giving equally impeccable evidence against you or me or anyone else who happens to have cramp in the left hand?

And next time, when it is not an archdeacon who is in the dock, are they going to be believed?

17 September 1978

***

Twice forty-five-year-old Mr Peter Adroni has been discharged from a bed in an 'acute ward' at St Bernard's Mental Hospital in Southall, Middlesex after having been declared sane and fit.

Twice he has been escorted to the gate by police and twice he has insisted on returning.

Do you blame him?

In a Britain in which citizens queue to give bottles of Scotch to striking firemen, and offer hardly a kind word to the soldiers who do their jobs, do you really blame anyone for deciding that the only sane place to be is inside a nuthouse?

27 November 1977

***

He would be a hard man who is not moved by the children's story written by Prince Charles 10 years ago for his younger brothers.

The tale shows sensitivity, imagination and humour. More important it reveals a deep and touching affection for the younger brothers the story was meant to entertain.

Can you imagine the average young man of twenty, which Charles then was, bothering to write fairy tales for kid brothers less than half his age?

The same love of family was mirrored in that one uncontrollable tear which filled his eye at Lord Mountbatten's funeral.

There are times when I feel that on the shoulders of the rest of us there ought to be a heavy burden of guilt that for many years to come and maybe for the rest of his life, we have consigned this marvellous young man, who has so much talent, so much creative ability and so much human warmth to being little more than a puppet who, with his hands behind his back, has to walk the stern, lonely, emotionless path of royal duty.

23 September 1979

It would appear that our Left-Wing Minister of Overseas Development, Mrs Judith Hart, has a taste for the good life.

It is just 3 weeks since she spent £12,000 of taxpayers' money entertaining overseas guests for a weekend in a four-star hotel to discuss 'the basic needs of the poor.'

Now we learn that £10,000 is to be spent on a loo next door to her office.

It is explained, of course, that the loo will not be for Mrs Hart's exclusive use.

Oh yes? Want to guess what would happen to any humble temporary typist found sitting on Mrs Hart's mink-lined throne and pulling Mrs Hart's golden chain?

1 October 1978

It is said that two members of the nursing staff of the Glasgow Royal Infirmary who helped in the abortion of a woman 24 weeks pregnant have had nightmares ever since.

I would not care all that much myself to see a perfectly-formed baby boy struggle to live for 10 minutes before being consigned to the dustbin.

But nightmares do not appear to trouble Professor Malcolm McNaughton who was responsible for permitting the abortion, and on grounds which medically are so far completely unexplained.

I watched him on TV dismiss with an arrogant wave of a hand any suggestion that the abortion was morally questionable. I note, however, that he himself was not present when it took place.

If he is willing to sanction the termination of a 24-week pregnancy shouldn't he at least have the guts to do the dirty deed himself?

28 October 1979

I marvelled again last week at the colours, the beauty and the wonderfully changing weather of my native heath.

There I was last Monday playing golf at Prestwick with people like Henry Cooper, Brian Barnes, Malcolm Gregson, Dickie Henderson and Dale Robertson, the Hollywood star of Wells Fargo.

At one moment we would be basking in sunshine and blue skies. The very next – and for half an hour at a spell – we would be literally on our knees cowering behind golf umbrellas in a vain attempt to protect ourselves from the hailstones beating in horizontally from the sea.

With a climate like that, is it any wonder that Scottish Nationalists want to keep the place to themselves?

1 October 1978

On 3 July at Wimbledon magistrates' court Mr Zenor Schramm, a British citizen of Polish descent, appeared on a charge of having used insulting behaviour while watching a match on No. 1 Court.

Evidence was given against him by two policemen.

I quote from that evidence: 'And the back of his right hand moved round the contours of her buttocks.'

Doesn't that sound familiar? Isn't it almost a re-run of what was said by the two policemen giving evidence against Archdeacon John Youens?

I will tell you something which is even more of a coincidence. The two policemen who gave evidence against the Archdeacon are exactly the same chaps who gave evidence against Mr Schramm.

As in the case of the archdeacon, not a word was heard from the girl against whom the offence was alleged to have been committed. There the resemblance ends. The Archdeacon was acquitted and now goes round with a halo above his dog collar. Mr Schramm, a family man with two children, was fined £50 and now has an indelible stain on his whole life and character.

Has justice been done? I do not know. I have no way of telling. But is it not monstrous that in both cases judgment should be passed without a word being heard from the girls alleged to have been insulted?

24 September 1978

He was a Roman Catholic priest, Irish. Aged about sixty.

He sat at the next table to me in a Soho restaurant. He looked frail. I overheard him tell his companion that he had risen from his sick bed.

But there was such an air of goodness, of serenity about him, such kindness, humanity and compassion in his craggy face that his very presence seemed to light up the whole restaurant.

I asked the waiter who he was and was told that he was a parish priest in North London and had been one for 40 years.

That was 3 weeks ago.

I went into the same restaurant the other night and asked about him again.

I was told that he had been buried that morning.

A moment of sadness? No.

My strong instinct is that there would have been a smile of happiness and contentment on that priest's face as he went to meet his God.

Can any man die poor who has a faith like his?

7 May 1978

It is suggested that Lady Falkender is about to change her political allegiance and move from the Labour to the Tory benches in the House of Lords.

Can it be true?

And if so, what is Marcia up to? Having fixed Sir Harold's position imperishably in history, is she now seeking to put the kiss of death on Mrs Thatcher?

8 October 1978

Professional boxing is not my favourite sport.

I am put off by the sight and sound of the ringsiders — many of them fur-coated, middle-aged women — baying for blood.

Well last week they had their blood all right. Angelo

Jacopucci, dead at the age of twenty-nine from a cerebral haemorrhage.

Who is to blame? Not Alan Minter. Least of all Alan Minter.

The punch with which he felled Jacopucci was only the culminating blow to a brain which had no doubt been savaged by similar punishment throughout the years.

If there is guilt at all, not only over Jacopucci but over all the other punch-drunk ex-professional boxers who stumble through the rest of their lives in a mental haze, it should be properly attached to the people who get a kick out of going to see other men bash each other about and the promoters who grow rich in catering for their sadism.

23 July 1978

■■—■■

Around 9.29 tomorrow morning, that super little chap Mr Sidney Weighell, Secretary of the NUR, fresh from his Blackpool triumph where he proved himself, not for the first time, to be the most courageous and most honest trade union leader in Britain, will be in the booking hall at Bishop's Stortford with eagle eye on the station clock.

He will be waiting for the magic moment of 9.30 a.m. when the cheap day tickets begin to operate.

Then Mr Weighell can travel to London for £1.95 second class return instead of £3.58.

Do I criticize him for the canny fashion in which he guards his bawbees?

No way.

Isn't it marvellous that at least he travels to and from work at his own expense instead of using, as I expect he could, a car and chauffeur provided by his union?

And wouldn't it be great if Cabinet Ministers had to travel the same way and were forced to experience the discomfort and cost which by their incompetence, they impose on the rest of us?

8 October 1978

··➤··

Mr J.A. Williamson, of Bexleyheath, Kent has a twenty-eight-year-old son in Rhodesia who has lost his job and can no longer support his wife and three young children.

The son wants to come home. The father desperately wants to have him home.

He scraped the money together and purchased air tickets to be made immediately available to his son in Salisbury.

But now the son has been informed by the British Consulate in Pretoria that he alone can travel home on his British passport, but not his wife and children who are Rhodesian-born.

Wonderful, isn't it, that this should be happening at the very same time that Mr Merlyn Rees is assuring Asians and other settled in this country that their wives, up to four per man in the case of Moslems, and dependant children will be allowed in without question?

30 July 1978

··➤··

In Washington, a twenty-two-year-old call girl, Miss Judy Chavez, tells us that everytime Russian defector Arkady Shevchenko slept with her he handed over £250.

And that in just 4 months she collected £20,000.

£250 a time? Is that really the going rate for sex in Washington.

I have not the slightest doubt that among the worthy kirk-going spinsters of Auchtermuchty this intelligence will have been received with pursed-lip disapproval.

But could there be other lassies, do you suppose, now thoughtfully looking up airline timetables?

15 October 1978

There are times when the willingness of Authority to take risks with the lives of innocent people makes your hair stand on end.

The Ministry of Health is for ever telling us that smoking is bad for our health. What do they think smallpox is?

How, then, can it happen that at a time when the disease has virtually been eliminated from the face of the earth experimenters were allowed to muck about with it in a laboratory in the middle of Birmingham?

And not only in Birmingham.

There is another smallpox laboratory, in St Mary's Hospital, Paddington – bang in the centre of London and close to a maternity unit.

Why?

If the smallpox virus has to be kept alive, why in crowded cities?

I do hope that that arch-prune Dr David Ennals is going to get on the box today and tell us.

3 September 1978

••➤••

At one moment in time there were 350 MPs in the Spanish Parliament all jabbering like mad in front of the TV cameras.

Then two or three shots were fired into the air and the very next second Parliament looked absolutely deserted as every single MP dived under his desk for cover.

In no way do I blame them. I would have been the first to get my head down.

But isn't it fascinating how, when it is their own skins they seek to save, fat and flabby politicians the world over can move even faster than the citizens of Auchtermuchty on a flag day?

1 March 1981

••➤••

<hr>

Can it really be true that the RAF has only seventy-four obsolescent aircraft to defend Britain?

Judging from the curiously evasive and embarrassed tone of official denials, I would suspect that the story is entirely true.

Still, isn't it a mercy to know that as long as we could count on our noble Prime Minister Mr Callaghan, and dynamic Defence Minister Mr Fred Mulley being personally in charge of the beach-head, we might still be able to ward off a rowing boat full of pregnant Pakistanis?

Provided of course that old Fred didn't drop off to sleep again.

3 September 1978

On any one day at the Hoover factory at Merthyr Tydfil, as many as 800 of the 5,200 workers are off sick.

Why? Is there some mystery malady sweeping South Wales?

Or might it have just something to do with the fact that the Hoover company pays the difference between sickness benefit and full wages? And that when transport costs are taken into account, it actually pays a man better to stay at home?

I do not know.

But isn't it a hoot that one laddie who, according to his medical certificate, should have been quietly dying at home, was caught out last week by being pictured instead in the local newspaper scoring the winning goal for his football team?

How much do you suppose he will be awarded in compensation for unfair dismissal?

15 October 1978

<hr>

No fewer than forty-eight ships ignored the frantic signals for help coming from the seventy-four Vietnamese refugees crammed together in the tiny 30-foot fishing boat drifting helplessly without food or water in the South China Sea.

Only two ships even bothered to stop.

One, a Chinese Communist ship, gave the refugees food, medical supplies and fresh water. I commend the Chinese for their humanitarianism.

The only other ship to stop, the Liberian ship *World Kingdom*, took the refugees on board and saved the fifty-four who were by that time still alive.

It is good to know that the captain of the *World Kingdom*, Captain Leslie Lawrence, is British.

But what about the masters of the other forty-eight ships?

Wouldn't it be wonderful to think that if ever they

themselves are drowning in the South China Sea, the only people to hear their cries of despair will be Vietnamese refugees packed in a fishing boat?

10 September 1978

There was one plaintive little plea last week that had me almost helpless with laughter.

It came from the seventy-year-old geezer caught with his pants around his ankles in the Streatham brothel where for £25 Mrs Cynthia Payne provided a meal and drinks, a blue film, a sex show and then a session in bed with one of the ladies in attendance.

'I'm a bit past it', he told police. 'I'm only here because it's a Christmas party.'

For that memorable remark, I would be prepared to forgive the ancient lecher almost anything.

I am much less forgiving about the hypocrisy and cant which surrounded the rest of the case.

What about the barristers, the solicitors, the business men, several vicars, the member of the House of Lords, the Republic of Ireland MP who were by no means past it and were found by police either in bedrooms with prostitutes or queueing up the stairs awaiting their turn in the bedroom?

If Mrs Payne has to face 18 months in jail and a fine of £1,950, why should they go scot-free?

Can't we even now at least have their names?

And if the threat of publicity is enough to make some South London vicars resolve henceforth to wear their trousers the same way round as their clerical collars, then all I can say is that it is high time they did.

27 April 1980

I was puzzled by the story of Mr Eugene Lambert, the Irish TV entertainer who was kept in a cell for 22 hours and whose family had to raise £20,000 to release him on bail.

The charge against Mr Lambert was that he had deserted from the British Army 34 years ago.

Thirty-four years ago? Are we really still hunting men who as youngsters committed that crime in the mists of time? Is it an offence that merits a bail level of £20,000?

And even if it had not been a case of mistaken identity, as it was with Mr Lambert, are we really daft enough to take action 34 years later against a citizen of Eire who if ever he had been in the British Forces would have been there as a seventeen-year-old volunteer?

4 May 1980

The sixty-six ladies who embarked on the Thames pleasure cruiser *Enchante* for 'A ladies' naughty hen night' knew precisely what to expect. And they got it.

They became hysterical with excitement when a male stripper called the Rhinestone Cowboy advanced upon them wielding a banana.

Weren't they wicked and wanton?

But if they go that mad over a banana, isn't it a mercy that their cabaret didn't have a kilted Reggie Bosanquet tossing the caber?

25 May 1980

The citizens of Llandudno have long been apprehensive about a depot containing 300 tons of liquid gas which Wales Gas set up in a residential area next door to a school and a hospital.

They became even more apprehensive after the recent Spanish camp-site tragedy.

There was a renewed clamour for its removal.

A local newspaper, the *North Wales Weekly News*, published a leader attacking the Gas Board under the headline 'Time To Put The Boot In'.

The moderately worded leader ended: 'The Gas Board, like the rest of our democracy, is more sensitive to successive kicks up its backside than to appeals to its better nature.'

Now on the extraordinary ground that the leader was an incitement to violence, the Gas Board has not only reported the newspaper to the Press Council but has also withdrawn advertising worth £200 a week.

Isn't it almost unbelievable that such crude blackmail should be practised?

Would they report me too if I were to suggest that Mr Dudley Fisher, the chairman of Wales Gas, should be kicked not just up the backside but right out of office?

10 September 1978

••◣►••

Two weeks ago I invited the Minister of Health, Mr David Ennals, to tell us why deadly live smallpox virus had been kept in the centre of Birmingham and still is being kept in the heart of London at St Mary's Hospital, Paddington, right next door to a maternity unit.

So far there has not been a squeak in reply.

Now, two quite unnecessary deaths later, I renew the invitation.

And when Mr Ennals does care to answer, as in the end he will have to, perhaps he will also tell just what experiments are being conducted with the virus; why such experiments are necessary; and whether, in the event of the virus escaping from Paddington, as it did from

Birmingham, he and the Prime Minister intend to accept full legal and moral responsibility.

17 September 1978

◗◖━◗◖

When Heckmondwike batsman George Muirhead was adjudged out l.b.w. for a duck in the Central Yorkshire League cricket match against Heckmondwike's deadly rivals, top of the table Altofts, he didn't like it at all. So he stayed at the crease.

And when told to 'Get on your bike' by opponent Clive Jackson, he responded by felling Mr Jackson with his bat.

Then he turned and felled the wicket-keeper too.

With a temperament like that, why on earth is he wasting his time playing Central Yorkshire League cricket?

Wouldn't he be a natural to take on John McEnroe at Wimbledon?

6 July 1980

◗◖━◗◖

I expect that somewhere on some TV screen the animal who murdered thirteen-year-old Carl Bridgewater watched the little coffin of his victim being lowered into the grave.

He would not have been moved, as the rest of us were moved, by the sight of Carl's little brother sobbing by the graveside.

For what he did he would have done deliberately knowing full well that in our crazy do-gooding society the punishment for shooting a thirteen-year-old boy is little more than that for fiddling income tax.

But the man who pulled the trigger at point blank range on little Carl was not alone at the time. There was a gang of three or maybe four involved. I cannot believe that they are all equally evil. There has to be one among them with some sort of conscience.

Why doesn't he relieve that conscience by going to the nearest telephone today and turning the murderer in?

1 October 1978

In Boots the chemists it was possible to buy for 75p children's sponges in the shape of a Golliwog.

Then came a solemn complaint from Mr Basil Manning, a member of the National Committee on Racism in Children's Books.

He saw the sponge as a symbol of racialism. Boots promptly caved in. There will be no more sponges.

Now Mr Manning strikes again. This time against the little paper Golly that for 50 years has been stuck on the side of every jar of Robertson's jam.

He threatens a boycott by blacks of the firm's products unless the Golly is removed.

Would it be too much to hope that Robertson's unlike

Boots, will have the guts to tell the insufferable Mr Manning and all the others like him to go and get lost?

6 March 1981

——

Doesn't the knighthood given to author Angus Wilson in the Birthday Honours List raise a slight problem?

Just a few years ago Mr Wilson spoke proudly of his sexual relationship with another man and told the world that they had just celebrated their twenty-fifth anniversary together.

May we expect that the Gay Liberation movement will now insist that we refer to his long-term live-in companion as Lady Wilson.

15 June 1980

——

Canon Keith Walker, the Precentor of Chichester Cathedral, defends the £45,000 grant which the World Council of Churches made to the terrorist forces in Rhodesia. He declares that he himself supports the guerrillas and that violence has to be met by violence.

Isn't that just a little bit odd coming from a chap who no doubt every time he enters the Cathedral bows towards the altar as a manifestation of his devotion to the Christian doctrines of gentleness, compassion and mercy and of his belief in Christ who said: 'Suffer little children to come unto me.'

Does he have even the slightest twinge of conscience at the thought that the £45,000 went to finance the monsters who far from suffering little children to come unto them attempted in the Elim Mission massacre to rape a four-year-old girl, kicked her in the face so savagely that the imprint of the heavy boot was still visible at the child's post mortem, bayoneted her in the arm and then no doubt just to make sure that she was really dead, crushed her skull.

I don't suppose for one second that he does.

But then I do not suppose he ever wonders either why, when there are prunes like him in the pulpits, the pews are so often so empty.

15 October 1978

━━━

On his way home from Exeter, *Sunday Express* colleague Iain Reid stopped for petrol at the Membury Service Station on the M4.

His first unpleasant surprise was the price of £1.47 a gallon. His second was when he tried to restart his car and failed.

He telephoned the AA from a kiosk in the service station but was informed that the AA could not come on to private property without the permission of the garage manager.

Since the garage office was on the other side of the motorway that involved a longish trek.

When he asked there whether he might call in the AA he received a short, sharp answer.

'No. Not until we have seen it first. It will cost you £7.50 plus VAT and if we can't get it started then you can call in the AA. We will come across and have a look at your car in about fifteen minutes.'

£7.50 plus VAT? Minimum? For a job which might have only taken 2 minutes?

As it happened, when Reid returned to his car and gave it a sharp angry kick, he was able to get it started by himself.

But isn't it a scandal that in addition to being a rip-off for petrol, motorway garages should be a rip-off in every other way too?

29 June 1980

[Editor's Note: The surprise would, of course, be even more unpleasant today.]

Mr Clive Jenkins suggests that the smallpox laboratory at Birmingham University may have been carrying out experiments which created a new and even more deadly type of smallpox virus.

Can this be true? Does this explain why the experts have not yet been able to identify the strain of smallpox that killed Janet Parker?

Could it even explain why one of the scientists involved committed suicide?

And if so, are similar experiments being carried out at St Mary's Hospital, Paddington, where, despite all the warnings he has been given, Mr David Ennals persists in maintaining live smallpox virus near a maternity unit?

22 October 1978

I bring you a little tale of high Socialist principle from Newport in Wales, a story of how the comrades of the valleys stood firm by the cause.

The Planning Committee of Newport Council had a meeting scheduled for 14 May last.

But that, as we all know, was the date chosen by Len Murray for his Day of Action – a day in which all true Socialists were to sacrifice a day's pay to show their solidarity.

Could the conflict be resolved? Yes indeed.

In early May the committee convened a special meeting to discuss whether or not they should hold their normal meeting on the Day of Action.

It lasted all of 10 minutes, and was attended by eleven councillors. They solemnly decided not to hold their normal meeting on 14 May.

Now three of these councillors have claimed attendance

allowance of £13.28 each for that 10-minute talk.

Would you be staggered to learn that first with his snout in the trough was the committee's Socialist chairman?

22 June 1980

When twenty-one-year-old Rhodesian Mr John Gardner looks into a mirror the reflection he sees is as black as the ten of clubs. Politically he is a supporter of Mr Joshua Nkomo.

So on both counts he is, at least in the eyes of Dr Owen, flawless. Isn't it a hoot then that had it not been for the personal panic-stricken intervention of the Minister, Mrs Judith Hart, Mr Gardner would have been deprived of the place provided for him at Keele University by the British taxpayer under the Overseas Development Ministry's Rhodesian African Training Programme?

Not because he is black. But because he is not black enough.

For Mr Gardner's paternal grandfather was Scottish. And therefore he is classified not as black but as coloured.

And Rhodesian coloureds, like Rhodesian Asians, like Rhodesian whites, are not eligible for any help.

Don't you call that racial discrimination?

And even if you don't, isn't it almost beyond belief that a black man may be deprived of help just because one-quarter of his blood may have started life behind a pair of visiting trews from Auchtermuchty?

22 October 1978

The two compassionate policemen who took sixty-seven-year-old dirty, unwashed vagrant Joseph Wilson to Hull Royal Infirmary in the early hours of a bitterly cold January morning did so because they were convinced that he was ill. But the doctor who examined him sent him packing.

The old tramp was too weak to walk far. He tottered 100 yards into the Infirmary car park.

He was seen there at 5 a.m. by the night porter.

When the day porter came on duty at 6 a.m. the night porter pointed out Mr Wilson lying on the frozen ground.

But it was not until 10 a.m. that the day porter went to investigate. He thought the tramp might be sleeping. He did not touch him.

But he did report the incident. Nothing was done. At one stage a casualty doctor who was asked to visit Mr Wilson refused to do so. It would have been too late anyway. The old tramp was very, very dead.

What have I to say about all this? Not a thing. Except that if ever I am old, and poor and feeble and found ill in Hull, I hope to God I have the good fortune to be taken to the local nick and not to the local infirmary.

26 February 1978

In my story last week of the old tramp who died from exposure after having been turned away from Hull Royal Infirmary in the early hours of a bitterly cold January morning, I did not give the name of the doctor who examined him.

It was Dr Falih Abed Ali Al-Fihan.

What was his nationality? I do not know. But I have a sneaking suspicion that he does not wear a kilt. And does not come from Auchtermuchty.

5 March 1978

The *Washington Post*, the American newspaper which exposed Watergate and destroyed President Nixon, has been telling a horrific story of an eight-year-old black boy who has been a heroin addict since the age of five.

The boy, who in the newspaper is called only 'Jimmy', began by sniffing the drug and now receives daily injections from his mother's lover.

The lover, a drug hustler, told a *Washington Post* reporter that Jimmy had been 'bugging him' about heroin shots and one day 'I let him snort a little, and damn, the little dude really did get off'.

And what does his mother, herself a heroin addict, say? She says: 'I think he would have got into it one day anyway.

The story of Jimmy is now arousing considerable anger in Washington. The authorities demand to know his name so that action can be taken against the parents, and the boy taken into care.

Incredibly the *Washington Post* refuses to give his name on the ground that to do so would be a betrayal of confidence, and cites that part of the US Constitution which protects the freedom of the Press.

Sad old world, isn't it when an editor is so proud of his principles and the integrity of his newspaper that he puts them before the life of an eight-year- old child?

For my own part I would rather make my living shovelling sewage in Swansea.

5 *October 1980*

[Editor's Note: Since this was written it has been shown that the story of Jimmy was invented by a *Washington Post* reporter.]

There are many things I will remember about my one-day visit to Aberdeen last Monday.

The view from my Dan-Air BA 111 of the coast by Stonehaven sparkling in the sunshine.

The rich, green Aberdeenshire fields and fat bellied Aberdeen cattle below me as we came in to land.

But most of all I will remember the blue eyes of the beautiful lassie, Selina Scott, who interviewed me for Grampian TV.

She made Angela Rippon and Anna Ford look like a couple of sock-knitting crones.

Is there a TV boss reading?

Why should the whole country be denied a sight which the people in the Grampian Region enjoy almost every evening?

27 July 1980

I can understand the shock suffered by twenty-four-year-old Mr David Burgin and his twenty-two-year-old wife Jacqueline when they returned just before midnight to their Crystal Palace flat to find their six-month-old baby whom they had left alone while they 'popped out' to a pub, had been savaged to death by the family's two pet ferrets — ferrets which had been left in the same room as the child and in an ill-secured cage.

I hope that shock will not be the only punishment they suffer.

Isn't jail the proper place for parents who leave a six-month-old child alone while they go off drinking?

29 October 1978

Mr Rod Stewart is, I note, called Phyllis by his friend, Mr Elton John.

Mr John answers in turn to Sharon.

Mr Stewart's manager has the pet name of Bridie.

Mr John's is called Beryl.

What sort of flowers do you suppose they send each other on their birthdays?

Pansies?

24 December 1978

●━━●

I can understand the jealous anger of Mrs Jean Harris, the fifty-seven-year-old upper-class headmistress who murdered her sixty-nine-year-old lover, Dr Herman Tarnower.

But it is the dead man whose last words, as she entered his bedroom and began to blaze away with her gun, were: 'Good God Jean, don't you realize it's the middle of the night?' who intrigues me.

He was the author of an internationally famous diet known as the Scarsdale diet and which consists largely of grapefruit and carrots.

He was also during the period of his affair with Mrs Harris having it off with thirty-five other women – some not much more than half her age.

Thirty-five women at the age of sixty-nine? Some of them still in their twenties?

And on grapefruit and carrots?

Isn't it a mercy for what was left of the flower of American maidenhood that no one ever introduced the old lecher to haggis and whisky?

1 March 1981

●━━●

Ahead of Mr N.J. Sullivan on the M1 north of Darlington a car hogged the fast lane. And like many of us in a similar situation Mr Sullivan became a mite irritated.

He flashed his headlights several times. The only response, according to Mr Sullivan, was that the other driver appeared to say something to his front seat passenger and then gestured rearwards with his thumb.

Finally, Mr Sullivan passed the car on the inside lane. As he did so he realized to his dismay that its occupants were uniformed police officers travelling in an unmarked police vehicle.

It must have been quite a traumatic moment. Nevertheless, Mr Sullivan continued his passing manoeuvre undaunted.

Subsequently, the police car overtook Mr Sullivan and, he tells me, remained in the offside lane until it turned off the motorway some 6 miles further on.

Mr Sullivan duly received a summons charging him with driving without due care and consideration. Last Thursday he was fined £40.

Just one thing puzzles me. If the police car was doing 70 mph and Mr Sullivan passed it why was he not charged with exceeding the speed limit? And if it was not doing 70 mph, why did it not move out of the outside lane when flashed?

Or is it really becoming police practice to try to goad drivers into breaking the law?

21 January 1979

So no one, but no one, was to blame for the life and death of Lester Chapman.

The very first time he ran away from home, in December 1977, a police doctor found eight weals on his right buttock and three on his left with the skin broken in some of the lesions. He referred to them as 'trivial' and so Lester was sent back to his mother and step-father, even though he begged not to be. The doctor is not even named in the report of the inquiry into Lester's death.

In the following 2 weeks Lester ran away from home three more times – and twice social workers sent him back. The social workers are exonerated.

On the day he ran away for the last time he told a little friend at school: 'I am going to the railways to get killed by a train . . . if I can't do that I want to run away.'

Poor little mite, whose body now lies under a heart-shaped headstone which proclaims how much his mother loved him.

What in God's name does an eight-year-old child in this country have to do before anyone listens to his cry for mercy?

21 October 1979

●━━●

I quickly discovered the big, burly, bearded Swiss whom unlucky chance had put by my side on the drag-lift which perilously pulled us up the mountain on skis, spoke no English.

I quickly discovered, too, that we were going to be in trouble on the icy hazardous track. His skis kept skidding into mine.

We were two thirds of the way up the mountain. On either side of the narrow track was snow 9 feet deep.

I calculated that if I fell off there I would probably still be in the same position when the edelweiss began to bloom.

Fortunately, it was not to be. For at that moment my companion gave a low moan, muttered something incomprehensible in Schweizer Deutsch, and fell backside first into the snow.

He was still there, on his back, his skis in the air, a sad reproachful look on his face, when I whizzed past some 20

minutes later. Charming, courteous people the Swiss. And at least one of them will know better next time than to share a drag-lift with any laddie who has ever caught the last bus from Auchtermuchty.

18 February 1979

In Dublin, the 900 mechanics, electricians and blacksmiths and bodymakers who maintain the city bus services are going to go on a 24-hour strike at midnight tonight as a protest against the refusal to give them free travel.

On Dublin's buses? No. No. On British Rail.

They cannot understand why they should be excluded from enjoying a perk which 'for historical reasons' so many of their colleagues including cleaners, have enjoyed for years.

Can their claim really be true? It can be and it is.

Isn't it marvellous that in addition to allowing the Southern Irish unrestricted entry into Britain and permitting them to vote in our elections, we can ferry a sizeable number of them here free and then provide them with complimentary tickets on our trains?

13 July 1980

It would not bother me much if I had been refused membership of the Irish Democratic League Club in Bradford.

Not even if I had been assured that most of the Irish had been kicked out because they made too much noise and that within the club's precincts scarcely a single Irish accent is now to be heard.

But it did bother Mr Chaganlal Mistry, an Indian and a practising Hindu. He went to court under the Race Relations Act demanding to have his barring set aside.

Isn't it wonderful?

But isn't the most hair-raising thing of all the fact that while Mr Mistry because of the colour of his skin, has the right to take legal action, that same right because of the colour of *their* skins is denied the poor old Irish drunks who have been tossed out on their white backsides?

15 June 1980

There are just one thousand ticket collectors at London's tube stations.

At the very least two out of three of them have to be honest men.

Which means that the remaining 300 have been fiddling £2½ million each year from the excess fares they collect.

£2½ million among just 300?

That is £8,000 tax free a head.

And since they work only 5 days a week and 48 weeks a year, I calculate that each single crooked ticket collector has been carrying home every night of his working life £34 in 10p and 5p pieces.

How in God's name do you suppose either their braces or their trouser pockets stand up to the strain?

4 March 1979

"━"

When John Stonehouse was granted his discharge from bankruptcy the other day it was disclosed that he has an index-linked parliamentary pension of £58 a week.

And that is after, not before tax.

£58 a week net, at the age of fifty-four? Index linked? For just 19 years' service?

Rum old world, isn't it when a crook who had to quit his job in disgrace should now be getting more than twice as much as an old-age pensioner who has toiled honestly for 50 years?

22 June 1980

"━"

Last Monday Jackie Stewart, who had just flown in that morning from New York, and I sat together at Wimbledon watching Bjorn Borg playing El Shafei.

Our attention was not focused all the time on the tennis.

We both found ourselves transfixed by a scene on the sidelines. There watching the play was Bjorn's fiancée, Mariana Simionescu, and Borg's coach, Lennart Bergelin.

The entire Centre Court audience applauded furiously every time Borg made a fine stroke. Miss Simionescu and Mr Bergelin never applauded once. Instead they chewed gum relentlessly, their jaws moving in absolute unison.

Said Jackie to me: 'My God, aren't they just about as dour as he is?'

And they were too.

Do you suppose the day will ever come again when men

and women at Wimbledon play tennis for the pride and honour of winning and not just for the commercial contracts and loot?

29 June 1980

Did you see the picture of sixty-one-year-old Dick Emery with his latest love, a gorgeous bird less than half his age, and almost twice his height?

Did you mark how she had her arm round his shoulder and a wonderful look of pride on her face as if to say 'Just look at what I've bagged'?

There are plenty of moralists who will deduce from the fact that Mr Emery has already been married five times that he is just a wicked old lecher.

Me? After a lifetime of observation of the Women's Institute in Auchtermuchty, I am more charitable.

My strong suspicion is that he is simply an ancient butterfly who for the sixth time in his life is soon going to be pinned to a board by a lassie who thinks faster and runs faster than he does.

Aren't women wonderful?

13 July 1980

Tory MP, Mr Christopher Brocklebank-Fowler has been boasting about how he can more than double his £10,725-a-year parliamentary salary by working just 3 hours a week at his own business as a marketing consultant.

Bully for him. It can't be bad to earn more per hour than even a Saturday NGA casual on *The Observer* newspaper.

But could Mr Brocklebank-Fowler now tell us how much of that money comes from Datsun, the Japanese car firm, for whom he acts as a consultant?

And by how much, if anything, his fees from Datsun

were increased after earlier this year he had described British Leyland cars as a load of junk?

6 March 1981

••➤••

When Peter Sellers suffered his first massive heart attack 16 years ago, I can imagine the advice which his doctors subsequently gave him.

'Take it easy old boy' they would have said 'and you can live to be a hundred. You are already a rich man. Why bother punishing yourself further in front of the film cameras?'

And what did Peter Sellers do? He continued to act as if there were no tomorrow.

He married yet another two beautiful birds – the last some 29 years younger than himself. He had affairs with some of the lovliest, leggiest fizzers in the world.

And when he wasn't making love, he was making people laugh with the genius of his acting.

On his morals I offer no judgment. But I admire his guts.

27 July 1980

••➤••

It must have been tough for Princess Anne to find herself publicly pilloried because she failed to show warmth to a small boy in hospital who was demanding to be cuddled and to have, as a result, angry Norwegians demanding that she go back to Britain.

I saw the incident on TV and I do not believe for one minute that the Princess acted with deliberate coldness. All she showed was her natural shyness and reserve.

Even so, and to prevent international incidents in future, might it not be wise when she goes on goodwill tours abroad if instead of visiting sick children in hospitals she contents herself with administering sugar lumps in stables?

No one is ever likely then to mistake the look of genuine love and compassion in her eyes.

12 November 1978

It is just as well that the Duchess of Windsor is old and frail and lives in France and was unable to see ITV's cruel portrayal of her love affair with the man who was once briefly our King.

Was she really such an unattractive, scheming bitch as depicted on the box? Did she really make trite, banal conversation in a voice that sounded like a nail being drawn across a slate?

Not as I remember her.

I met her only once. As a young man at a time when she was already middle-aged. I sat next to her at a private dinner party in the South of France.

I came away from that dinner enchanted by her warmth and her charm and the quality of her mind. I also began to understand why the man across the table had given up his throne for her. She was very far removed from the lady of last week for whom no man in his senses would have given up a bag of potato crisps.

It may be that my judgment of the Duchess was wrong. But even if it were, could they not at least have waited until she was dead before enriching themselves by lampooning her so viciously?

12 November 1978

In Tyneside, a retired headmaster, Mr W.H. Strachan, had the touching idea of offering three prize funds of £100 each to local schools to commemorate three Coldstream Guardsmen – one of them his own brother — who died on active service.

One of the £100 prizes was to be known as the Guardsman Stanley Strachan prize, another was to be named after Corporal William Dobson, VC and the third was to be the Guardsman Henry Creighton Cockburn award.

Was his offer accepted with acclamation? No.

The schools sub-committee of the Socialist-controlled North Tyneside Council was willing to accept the money but not the names, and suggested that Mr Strachan re-designate the prizes. Because as one Labour councillor explained: 'We are against militarism: we are frightened of militaristic values.'

A strange, sad country isn't it when awards to commemorate the achievements of hot-air merchants like Harold Wilson and Anthony Wedgwood Benn would be eminently acceptable, while prizes to commemorate three brave soldiers should be looked upon as badges of shame?

3 August 1980

At the reception given for Prince Philip in the British Embassy in Moscow members of the embassy staff were precisely primed by a circular on how to conduct themselves.

They had to stand in little groups, each with an appointed leader, behaving and talking in the most natural way until the moment Prince Philip arrived anywhere near them. They were then to put down their drinks and cigarettes, the ladies to make a half-curtsy and the men a little bob of the head. Then they were to stand there waiting for Prince Philip to say something.

And no doubt to fall about laughing when he did.

Do you really blame Prince Philip if in these circumstances and constantly surrounded by audiences like that, he sometimes acts and talks as if he were the greatest comic since Harry Lauder?

11 March 1979

The spectacle of Kenyan Asian Mr Jaffer Janmohamed and his four children being chased across London by reporters and cameramen eager to chronicle the family's quest for free board and lodging at the expense of the British taxpayer should afford no pleasure to anyone.

The Janmohamed family who arrived here with just £13 are completely innocent. They were only exercising their rights. Throughout the world it is known and accepted as Holy Writ that any family entitled to enter Britain does so with a guarantee of accommodation and a job or Social Security.

Yet how can Hillingdon Council which refused to house them and dumped them instead at the front door of the Foreign Office be considered guilty either? Why should any council ask its ratepayers to shoulder the financial burden of a Government policy which, in giving homeless immigrants preference over homeless Britons, offends natural justice?

On their first night here the Janmohameds were put up in an hotel by a housing charity.

Strange, isn't it, that neither our Foreign Secretary Dr David Owen nor our free-spending Minister of Overseas Development Mrs Judith mink-lined-loo Hart were on hand to put their homes where their mouths are and offer the family at least temporary personal hospitality?

12 November 1978

That very nice man, and devout Roman Catholic, Mr Norman St John Stevas tells us that before setting out on a journey he always gets down on his knees and prays for a safe trip and a safe return. As an extra insurance he wears under his semmit a medal of Our Lady.

I applaud his faith. But a prayer every time he sets out on a journey?

Isn't that overdoing it just the teeniest little bit?

Still at least I begin now to understand why the Good Lord paid so little attention to my own pitiful pleas for mercy when I crossed the Channel in my own little boat in a gale last week.

How could He when He is permanently in dialogue with Norman?

26 August 1979

Did you mark the name of the one leading British Politician who went to Claridge's to pay his respect to Richard Nixon on the ex-President's first day in London?

You may well have missed it.

So I will give you a clue.

It was a former Prime Minister who, as far as honour and integrity are concerned, stands head and shoulders above all other Prime Ministers of our generation.

You are, of course, no longer in doubt.

Lord Home.

Showing, as he always has, the same friendship to a man when he is down as when he is up.

Aren't there times when, like me, you wistfully speculate as to where this nation might be today if 14 years ago we had turned to Alec Douglas-Home instead of James Harold Wilson?

3 December 1978

As I drove back to London down the M6 and M1 the other day in gale-force winds and driving rain, I reflected that I would have been safer flying a light aircraft in thick fog.

My admiration went out to the heavy lorry drivers, tail to tail, mile after weary mile.

We private motorists travel in these suicidal conditions only occasionally. And usually from choice.

They face the dangers almost every day of their lives. And because they have to.

No matter how much we pay them, it will never be enough.

17 December 1978

It must have been quite a night at the Tatler Cinema Club in London's Stockwell Green when a stripper giving a performance between the showing of two pornographic films and on the very point of removing her G-string was attacked by a man who lumbered on the stage and tried to make love to her.

The man, twenty-five-year-old Mr Cleveland Lindo, was found guilty of assault but the sentence was deferred while the Recorder of London considered the matter.

Now, after a month of deliberation, he has been placed on 2 years' probation, which suggests the judge may have thought he was provoked.

The stripper remains anonymous. All we know about her is that she is now a school teacher.

A school teacher?

Just what is she teaching and to whose innocent children?

And how do you suppose she now spends her Sundays? Banging the cymbals in a Salvation Army band?

25 March 1979

Remember Mr Jaffer Janmohamed? He was the pathetic Kenya Asian widower who on 5 November last, arrived at Heathrow Airport with his four children and just £13 and demanded his right to a house and Social Security.

The Tory council at Hillingdon, fed up with housing penniless immigrants, dumped them on the doorstep of the Foreign Office. Subsequently Socialist Wigan offered them a council house.

There is now more news of Mr Janmohamed.

He has lit off from Wigan leaving his four children behind. The tenancy of the council house has been signed over to his eldest son, Riaf, a twenty-year-old student.

The £9-a-week rent for the house is still being paid out of Social Security, as no doubt are the tuition fees for Riaf, and the food, clothing and spending money of the family.

Where exactly is Mr Janmohamed himself? No one knows for sure. Although one report has it that he was married in January in London to a woman with business interests in Tanzania where the happy couple may now be living.

If true, have we then seen the last of him? I very much doubt that. He is still only forty-five. Want to bet than in another 20 years he will turn up again with another four children to dump on us? And in his hot little hand an application for an Old Age Pension?

25 March 1979

••══••

I accept that modern medicine is wonderful.

But all my alarm bells start ringing at the story of thirty-five-year-old Michael Taylor, who after a church exorcism service killed his wife by tearing out her eyes and tongue in 1975 and was sent to Broadmoor.

Isn't it just about the biggest miracle since Lazarus that just 3 years later Mr Taylor should now be pronounced cured, released from Broadmoor, and sent to lead a normal life in a Bradford suburb?

It may be, of course, that on this occasion, unlike many others, the doctors happen to be right.

But if they are not right, are they and Home Secretary Mr Merlyn Rees, who sanctioned Michael Taylor's release, willing to accept responsibility if he should decide to marry again and attend another exorcism service?

7 January 1979

••══••

Not once in my puff have I ever been asked my views by a poll of public opinion.

Nor have I ever met anyone who has.

Why the hell, then, should we pay so much attention to what the polls say? The people who do the actual questioning may be utterly conscientious – although it must be added that were they not, their capacity to influence events could be enormous.

They could by indicating a swing to one party or another actually create that swing.

Why don't we end that influence? Not by banning polls but by simply making sure that if ever we do happen to be questioned, we say the exact opposite of what we actually believe.

Who knows? We might even end up with a breed of politicians who say and do what they think right. And not just what they think will produce the most favourable reaction from the next findings of Dr Gallup.

1 April 1979

Ronald Leighton battered his three-month-old twins so severely that one of them suffered brain damage and will be blind for the rest of his life. His twin sister was luckier. She only had broken ribs.

For that dreadful offence Leighton was sent to jail for only 14 months.

Why?

It may be that the judge was influenced by the fact that Leighton, just twenty-three, had already spent 3 years in jail.

With two other juveniles he was convicted of murder when he was fifteen. There was subsequent doubt about the circumstances in which the youths confessed and 4 years ago, on that technicality, the conviction was quashed.

So the judge may have thought that he has had a rough deal.

But hasn't his three-month old son had a rougher one?

What is to happen to that mite and his little sister when their father is again free, as I expect he will be, just 10 more months from now?

16 September 1979

••◄━••

Not for one second did the staff of the National Westminster Bank in Western Avenue, East Acton, hesitate when two men carrying sawn-off shotguns burst in and demanded that a door leading behind the counter be opened.

With one accord they dived under the counter and hid there, bravely defying the gunmen's threats to shoot three women customers unless the door was opened.

Am I criticizing them? In no way. Had I been there I would have been the first to dive.

But if the bank, thankful that the raid was foiled, is to give a reward, may I suggest that it go to the three ladies who found themselves on the wrong side of the counter and at the wrong end of the sawn-off shotguns?

18 March 1979

••◄━••

Lesley Hendry was just two months old when she died.

She had twenty-seven fractures of the ribs, a broken leg, a torn liver and a head wound.

The jury was told that her father, twenty-five-year-old Graham Hendry, had battered the child because she cried with colic; that he had squeezed her until she went limp, punched her in the stomach, hurled her into her cot, held her upside down by her ankles and repeatedly shaken her.

Yet he walked free from the dock to be greeted with a

hug and kiss from his wife who in 6 weeks is expecting their second child.

How could it happen? Was it in part because the judge accepted the defence argument that there was no need for a custodial sentence since doctors and social workers would keep a close eye on the second child?

If so, what is going to happen if, in the middle of the night, the new baby has colic and there is no watchful doctor or social worker in attendance?

17 May 1981

It is natural that our new Archbishop of Canterbury, Dr Robert Runcie, should seek to win over the young by presenting a vigorous and sporting image.

But may I offer him a word of friendly advice?

The young are not likely to be attracted by the publicity pictures taken last Sunday of him playing tennis in baggy shorts which came down to his knobbly knees and socks which almost joined them. Nor are they likely to be impressed by his holding a racket more as if he were about to catch a butterfly than hit a tennis ball.

The harsh truth is that they are more likely to titter.

Dr Runcie will do much better if, like the Pope, he attracts the young by simply preaching the word of God.

16 September 1979

It must have been a revealing moment for his fellow first-class passengers when the Rt Hon. Anthony Wedgwood

Benn lost his cool on learning that because of staff shortages there would be no restaurant car on the 8.55 a.m. from Euston to Manchester.

I would have lost my own cool at being deprived of my porridge, bacon and egg.

But Wedgie? Isn't anger at the failure of railway staff to turn up for duty a little surprising coming from someone who has given up his title, his middle name, his entry in *Who's Who* – almost everything, in fact, except his own and his wife's money – to prove that he is a true member of the proletariat?

What was he doing travelling first class at all? Wouldn't he have better preserved that carefully cultivated image by sitting in the guards van with a Thermos and sandwiches?

30 September 1979

Last May I told the story of how Caroline Kitson daughter of Sedgefield District Council's Socialist chairman, John Kitson, had been appointed to a £4,000-a-year council job which required a driving licence even though she did not drive.

There was a bit of a fuss at the time. The job was re-advertised and new interviews held. Miss Kitson, who had by that time passed her driving test, still got the job.

Now I report that another of Mr Kitson's daughters is working for the council.

How many children has Mrs Kitson? Four.

When they all have jobs with Sedgefield District Council, do you suppose there will be any room left for his nephews and nieces?

21 October 1979

For nearly 3 years consultant surgeon Brian Hamilton pleaded for a vital piece of equipment for his orthopaedic hospital that would cost just £800. No dice. For 5 years he and other consultants dreamed of an X-ray machine that would cost £15,000 and with which the time of some operations could be cut from 2 hours to 20 minutes. No chance. Yet in the same hospital the local health authority sanctions a rest room for administrative workers at a cost of £12,000.

Comforting, isn't it, to know that while we deny patients in pain the chance of health, at least we have the decency to provide the administrative workers with comfortable rest rooms in which to sip their coffee?

19 March 1978

On Wednesday thirty-eight Manchester councillors and officials fly to Stuttgart on an overnight trip for which ratepayers will pick up the air and first-class hotel bills.

Why are they going?

Because Manchester has to decide whether to build a new runway at the city airport or to close the airport for two months to remake the existing runway.

Stuttgart faced the same problem several years ago and closed down. Now Manchester wants to know how it fared.

But isn't it a hoot that it should take thirty-eight delegates to travel all that way to find out what could have been sent by post on one sheet of foolscap?

20 November 1977

Lucky chap, Mr Anthony Johnson.

There he was just 2 years ago so ill with an unspecified

complaint that he had to leave his job as secretary to Hampshire County Council at the early age of forty-two.

On the strength of a note from his personal doctor he was given a golden handshake of £8,000 and an inflation-proof pension of £100 a week.

It seemed only a matter of time before the chaps in the black top hats would be moving in on him, carrying the oak box with brass handles.

Yet within months, and after a recovery swifter than if the Blessed Virgin had touched him, Mr Johnson became a lecturer at Southampton Polytechnic which is partly funded by the same council. Then about 18 months ago he was made the £11,500 head of legal services for the Welsh Land Authority.

When he comes to retire from that job, he will be due for a further inflation-proof pension.

All absolutely legal. All above board.

But isn't it a wry thought that there are still some of the Great Train Robbers in jail after having taken, by comparison, only peanuts from the public purse?

11 December 1977

When Mr Fred Mulley visited Saudi Arabia last September, he was accompanied by six officials and three Service Officers from the Ministry of Defence.

Mr Mulley presented gifts, paid for by the British Taxpayer, to his host Prince Sultan bin Abdul Aziz al Saud.

In return the Prince Sultan presented Mr Mulley with a gold and diamond Piaget watch worth £3,000 and each member of his party with a Rolex Oyster wrist-watch worth £300.

There was an extra little titbit for Mr Mulley, a gold and jewelled dagger worth about £9,000.

How much Customs duty has been paid on that little lot?

Not a penny.

The customs decided that no duty was necessary provided 'the items in question are retained by the individuals to whom they were given and not disposed of in any way'.

Interesting phraseology, isn't it? Yet when I telephone one of Mr Mulley's staff – a chap who was himself on the receiving end of a Rolex Oyster – I was assured, after what seemed to me to be some seconds of surprise and hurried consultation, that never, ever could there be any chance of the gifts becoming the personal property of those to whom they were given.

Really? Even when the Customs ruling specifically stated otherwise?

I do hope that by bringing the matter into the light of day I have not ruined poor old Fred Mulley's Christmas.

I also hope he does not do anything desperate with that gold and jewelled dagger.

18 December 1977

Mr Rod Stewart prides himself on waving the flag for Scotland.

I wish he wouldn't. I have seen better advertisements for my native country lying in the gutter in Maryhill Road on a Saturday night.

The conduct of Mr Stewart and his party of thirteen fellow morons on a DC10 from Los Angeles to London was nothing short of appalling.

Even more appalling perhaps is the fact that British Airways have not had the guts to say that they will never fly the drunken bum again.

Before I leave Master Stewart, I remark on one further thing.

As he tripped off the DC10 waving a whisky glass in his

hand, he confessed that he has to get well 'tanked up' before he can go on stage to sing.

That I can understand.

I would have to be well 'tanked up' before I would want to listen to him.

1 January 1978

Did the citizens of that Socialist paradise of mid-Glamorgan, where the song of the mavis can now hardly be heard above the rustle of notes being stuffed into councillors' wallets, think that because I have not written about them for a while, I had forgotten them?

Did local magistrate Councillor Robert Reed imagine that I had abandoned him?

Never, ever.

Mr Reed is the chap, you may recall, who once went on a free Concorde flight to Newfoundland, at a time when many would have given an eye tooth even to see the plane, had a slap-up-meal, and on his return had the crust to claim £10 attendance money. He is also the fellow whose council expenses and allowances were at that time, 1975, averaging £54 a week.

I now report that Mr Reed has not lost his touch. In the last set of figures for mid-Glamorgan councillors' expenses he is still right at the top. In the 6 months ending last September he collected £1,760.04 – an average of £67.69 a week.

Not bad, is it, especially when on top of all this he works for the Coal Board? Do you suppose he gets free coal too?

1 January 1978

Mr William Robinson must have been a real sanctimonious old so-and-so.

There he was spouting like a Holy Willie as a Methodist lay preacher on Sundays, and every other day of the week robbing the till of the Wakefield Building Society.

Nor did he even have the good taste to spend the lolly – some £134,000 of it over 30 years – on sensible things like wine and women.

The silly old fool spent it filling in the pools.

Can you beat it?

Yet even more extraordinary is that in his sinning Mr Robinson was only trudging down an already well-trodden path.

In this century, up until 1976, the Wakefield Building Society had only four general managers. The only honest one held the job for just 4 years.

Of the others the first went to jug for 5 years in 1907.

Another, Mr George Eli Jackson, general manager from 1911 to 1949, died owing the society £252,000.

Then came Mr Robinson.

Doesn't it set an alarm bell clattering in your mind?

Was the Wakefield Building Society unique?

Or can there be other building society managers who spend every Sunday in the pulpit and the rest of the week filling in the Treble Chance?

22 January 1978

───

In my time I have been called many things. But never before a racist.

Yet that is how I have been branded by the Press Council because I had said of a doctor who, after the most cursory examination turned away a dying tramp from Hull Infirmary, that although I did not know his nationality, with a name like Dr Falih Abed Ali Al-Fihan I did not think he wore a kilt or came from Auchtermuchty.

Do I now bow my head in penitence? Like hell.

I would say exactly the same again.

But I tell you this. Even if Dr Falih Abed Ali Al-Fihan spends the rest of his life turning away dying tramps, I think I will still have more respect for him than I have for the po-faced, pompous, pin-striped, humourless twits who sit on the Press Council.

3 September 1978

I have not the faintest idea whether fifteen-year-old Bassey Duke was the black youth who tried to rape a Miss X near Glasgow University on 22 March.

But I do remark that at an identification parade in which Miss X was invited to point out her assailant, Master Duke was the only black person present.

Isn't that, even for Scotland, just a little bit hot?

Or do the Glasgow police expect me to congratulate

them for the fair play and sense of justice they showed by not having the others dressed up in kilt and sporran?

11 December 1977

It must have been a wonderful moment for fifty-one-year-old Jimmy Beaton when he met and chatted with the Queen when she came to inaugurate the Aberdeenshire gas terminal where he works.

For is he not the father of Princess Anne's personal detective Inspector James Beaton, who was wounded thrice when a gunman attacked Princess Anne?

And might he not have expected that Her Majesty would have a word to say about what his boy had done?

But on that particular subject she said nothing at all.

In no way do I blame the Queen. She has to shake hands with thousands of people every year.

But might there not have been someone on her staff to advise her just how much a word of appreciation would have meant to the father of the young man who almost gave his own life to save Princess Anne's?

14 May 1978

It is of course a marvellous gimmick of Miss Tunisia to wear a yashmak and prevent our seeing her face.

Showing only her eyes she contrives to look a damn sight more exciting and more alluring than most of the other Miss World contestants.

Wouldn't it be marvellous if the idea were to catch on and some British ladies hid their faces too?

I can think of nothing more soothing.

Especially on my morning train to London.

12 November 1978

Mr Rod Stewart, the laddie who not so long ago had to be poured out of the first-class cabin of a British Airways DC10, clearly regards himself as one of the world's great lovers.

Hark to his conceit: 'I have always been the one to say "Sorry, that's it darling. It's all over. Goodbye".'

And about Miss Britt Ekland he says that when he walked out on her, 'I completely crushed her world'.

Just who does he think he is kidding?

Does he really delude himself that Miss Ekland, or indeed any of his other long-legged expensive lovelies, would even give him the time of day, far less a whiff of her deodorant, were it not for the millions he had made?

If ever a band struck up an old-fashioned Lady's Choice I doubt whether with his looks, his charm and without his lolly, Mr Stewart would ever get asked to jig. Not even, God help him, in the Women's Rural Institute in Auchtermuchty.

2 April 1978

Eyebrows are being raised because forty-three-year-old Lord Brooke keeps flogging off priceless Canalettos, Van Dycks, Rubenses, and other treasures from Warwick Castle.

It is suggested that in doing all this Lord Brooke is not quite playing the game. There is even tut-tutting that because he lives in France he does not have to pay capital gains tax.

Why the hell should he? And why should anyone complain about what Lord Brooke does? Don't the pictures belong to him? And has he not a right to do exactly what he wants with them? Besides, who other than a nutcase, would want to keep them in his own private possession when they are bound to end up, one way or another, being confiscated by a Socialist or maybe even a Tory Chancellor of the Exchequer.

26 March 1978

$ →→ $$

Without question I accept that a building society is the safest place for your lolly.

And that 99.99 per cent of building society bosses will end up as altar boys in heaven.

But my golly, don't the other .01 per cent have a ding-dong of a time?

Isn't it fantastic that dull, old, respectable seventy-nine-year-old Harold Jaggard should have gone through seven million quid of Gray's Building Society cash in 30 years?

It makes the £600,000 which, as recently disclosed, successive general managers of the Wakefield Building Society managed to get away with over 30 years look like peanuts.

But then they, of course, were only filling in football pools. Mr Jaggard, it would appear, had blondes as well as bookies.

Heigh-ho! It all goes to prove, I suppose, that it is every bit as dangerous to assess a man's honesty by the cut of his striped pants, as it would be to judge a spinster's passion by the thickness of her winter woollies.

2 April 1978

If I, like Mr Ludovic Kennedy, had been turned down previously by Muirfield Golf Club, I think I would have got the message.

Mr Kennedy is made of sterner stuff.

On his second attempt, he had as sponsors two former club captains.

Are these two men now themselves going to resign from

the club which has spat not just in their nominee's face but also in their own? I would hope so.

Besides, who would want to remain a member of the club which, by rejecting an interesting chap like Mr Kennedy, reveals itself as a bunch of dull sanctimonious, po-faced Scottish legal creeps?

Do you suppose Muirfield would have dared to do the same thing if Mr Kennedy instead of being a TV personality had been a Pakistani shopkeeper?

9 April 1978

••━••

I congratulate Mr Terry Wogan on having achieved the supreme accolade of being chosen to appear on his fellow Irishman Eamonn Andrews's programme *This is Your Life*.

It must have been quite a moment for all Mr Wogan's relatives who were flown over from Ireland to take part.

Good luck to them. May the blessings of the Liffey be upon them all.

But can you imagine an English disc-jockey being similarly lionized by an English commentator in Dublin?

23 April 1978

••━••

I have no complaint to make about the 9 month suspended sentence imposed on Caerphilly Rugby player John Billinghurst who, in an off-the-ball incident, punched an opponent on the face so viciously that he broke the man's jaw in two places and caused him to be off work for 9 weeks.

But one thing does mystify me. After the case was over the man whose jaw was punched, Mr George Grist, said: 'I did not start the prosecution and I did not want it. It could change the whole game of Rugby and I am sorry it ended in court.'

Aren't these curious words? 'It could change the whole game of Rugby.'

If Rugby is indeed played in this fashion, isn't it about time it was changed?

18 June 1978

—

To the news that in Saudi Arabia drinking alcohol is punishable by flogging and adultery by death, I had only one reaction.

Isn't it a mercy that the World Cup was not staged in Riyadh?

If it had been, and all the stories about the high jinks in hotel bedrooms are true, then I very much doubt if even twenty-two pairs of baggy pants would ever have arrived safely back home in Bonnie Scotland.

18 June 1978

—

Did you remark that on the TV pictures of the wedding of Princess Caroline, Princess Grace looked young enough and beautiful enough to be the bride's sister?

And that fifty-five-year-old Prince Rainier looked old enough and shagged-out enough to be the grandfather of them both?

Is it just possible that being the wife of a Ruritanian prince is a damned sight less exhausting than being the husband of a glamorous, exciting former Hollywood film star?

2 July 1978

—

Mr Dennis Skinner, the loud-mouthed ultra Left-wing Socialist MP for Bolsover, was swift to recognize the smelly substance hurled at him and other MPs from the public gallery of the House of Commons.

But then didn't he start with an advantage? Hasn't he been talking it for years?

9 July 1978

■■━■■

When two local GPs, Dr Syed Ahsan and Dr Chatur Shivnani, saw eleven-year-old Samuel Davis they pronounced that he was only constipated.

When his mother took him to St Leonard's Hospital, in London's Hoxton, and pleaded with the staff to admit her son because she was sure he was dying, the casualty officer, Dr Jillian Farrer, pronounced that he had only a virus infection and turned him away.

The little chap had to be supported to the nearest bus stop by his parents.

Twelve hours later he died from a ruptured appendix.

Marvellous Health Service isn't it, when without the fear of real punishment the two GPs concerned will happily go on prescribing Ex-Lax and the casualty doctor will still presumably go on turning away eleven-year-old appendicitis sufferers, provided they still have enough life left in them to be carried to the nearest bus stop?

16 July 1978

■■━■■

For at least 10 days and possibly a damned sight longer President Carter, Comrade Brezhnev and the political leaders of every major country in the world knew that an atomic-powered Soviet spy satellite was out of control and heading for earth.

Yet during that period, ordinary people heard not a dicky-bird.

We are now told that the silence was for our own good, to prevent our panicking.

Now wasn't that kind of our masters?

We are also now told that there was never at any time the slightest danger. Really? When it is clear that they had not the faintest idea where it would land?

And what is going to happen next time, and there will be a next time, if it is not Canadian wasteland but Paris or New York or Berlin or London or Glasgow that is at the receiving end?

Are some of us going to meet our Maker with a look of open-eyed amazement on our faces while the really important people like Mr Callaghan and Mr Michael Foot are down on their knees in bomb-proof shelters?

29 January 1978

That Mr Thomas Frazer, a fifty-six-year-old East London vagrant, was feeling out of sorts is understandable. His skull was fractured.

There is evidence that late at night he had been trying unsuccessfully to make his own way to the casualty department of Hackney Hospital.

The next day after having collapsed in the street he was taken there by ambulance.

And after an examination was told to push off. He did so. Only to collapse and to be carted back yet again.

This time the hospital called the police. Possibly, I suspect, because Mr Frazer smelled of drink.

The police refused to arrest him because they did not believe he was drunk. Instead they took him and left him to sleep on a bench in a nearby graveyard. One policeman cared enough to return to the graveyard to find out how he was. But by that time it was too late.

A doctor told the inquest that the hospital thought Mr Frazer had been drinking. But what if, to relieve his pain, he had been?

Is medicine in Hackney in such a primitive state that it is impossible to tell the difference between a hangover and a fractured skull?

And am I going to be reported to the Press Council if I say that the name of the doctor who gave the evidence was not McTavish and that he certainly didn't come from Auchtermuchty?

29 October 1978

In his will Sir Neville Cardus left £30 for a dinner party for his close friends.

Cardus was not a wealthy man. But, even so, the amount by present standards is derisory. It would hardly buy twenty friends a pint of beer and a ham sandwich.

The explanation probably is that Cardus made his will some years ago.

And yet, could there not be another explanation?

How many real friends, as opposed to acquaintances has any man?

For most of us, even at today's prices, wouldn't £30 still be enough to cover the bill?

25 May 1975

•◄••►•

I wonder exactly what the purpose is of the scarifying TV advertisement which shows a sickly premature baby lying on a cot.

Two students looking at him are saying: 'Poor little chap.'

A doctor says: 'He is luckier than the other ones who die.'

The students then ask: 'Couldn't anything have been done?'

The doctor replies: 'Yes. At least the mother should have stopped smoking when she was pregnant.'

Can you imagine the effect an advertisement like this must have on the woman who smokes a few cigarettes a day and is already well advanced in pregnancy?

And is there any positive evidence to support the propaganda being pushed out? Not one iota.

Perhaps the worst aspect of all is that this pernicious and harmful and tasteless propaganda is being paid for out of public funds.

2 March 1975

•◄••►•

On a visit to London from his home town of Aberdeen, old Frederick Sandison picked up a blonde widow and went back to her bed-sitting room for a 'kiss and cuddle'. For the next 10 years after that first meeting in the 1960s he kept coming to London three or four times a year for more of the same. And every time of course he dipped into his sporran and gave the lass a few bawbees.

Last week he failed in a court action to have the money returned.

There is an old Scottish saying that 'Ye canna tak the breeks off a Hielander.'

Seventy-nine-year-old Mr Sandison surely proves that if the Hielander comes from Aberdeen and you do succeed in taking his 'breeks' off, he will do his damnedest to get them back on again.

29 June 1975

A choir of American school children fly from Minnesota to Scotland to sing for Christian unity.

All starry-eyed and innocent.

In Glasgow they are received ecstatically. But afterwards they are told that they have been banned from a parish church in Inverness.

Why? Because it has been discovered that out of the thirty-two, eight are Roman Catholics. And the Presbyterian minister wants nothing to do with RCs. Not even school children.

Isn't it enough to make you weep?

Still if I were the eight young Americans, I wouldn't be too upset about not having been allowed into the church concerned.

It doesn't sound as if God has been allowed in there either for a long, long time.

29 June 1975

When it comes to putting the boot in, there is no one quite like a woman.

Did you read Mrs Harold Pinter's remark that although her husband had left home without a change of clothing, he would not have to worry about a change of shoes?

'He can always wear some of Antonia's. She has very big feet, you know.'

Isn't that a hat pin straight in the backside?

I suspect that from now on nobody will ever look at Lady Antonia's face. They will all be too busy peeping at her size eleven's.

3 August 1975

11◀▬▶11

Mr Arthur Scargill is not, I imagine, being deliberately offensive when he tells us that after the Communists have taken over in Britain a job serving in Woolworths will be found for the Queen. Just being his normal courteous self.

Just giving us a true picture of what life would be like in the miserable egalitarian Britain he and the comrades plot and plan. But if in fact the day ever comes when Her Majesty is serving in Woolworths, who do you suppose will be waving from the balcony at Buckingham Palace?

Arthur Scargill?

10 July 1977

11◀▬▶11

Cardinal Heenan was a prince of the Roman Catholic Church.

Yet when he died he left only £3,459.

Had he lived longer he would almost certainly have given even that away. His only provision for retirement was his old-age pension.

I do not suggest that poverty is necessarily synonymous with godliness. Or wealth with evil. But wouldn't it be nice to think that one day an Archbishop of Canterbury will die as poor and beloved as Cardinal Heenan?

11 July 1976

I always knew that Gee's Linctus was just the job for tickly tonsils.

But isn't it fascinating that after having swigged the linctus, Mr Brian Yeo should have been acquitted of

drunken driving? For it would appear that in every bottle there is the equivalent of one and a half glasses of whisky.

If the defence of drinking Gee's succeeded for Mr Yeo, how can it fail for anyone else?

I tell you this. From now on there is likely to be an awful run on the stuff in Fleet Street.

5 March 1978

I am all for protecting the young.

But I am in two minds about the sentence of a year in jail imposed on the forty-two-year-old unemployed Oldham builder who found himself the prize when his twenty-six-year-old wife and her two teenage sisters sat down to play rummy.

The winner of the game was his wife's fourteen-year-old sister – a busty, precocious lass. She claimed her prize, led her brother-in-law upstairs, removed her own and his clothing and forced herself upon him.

Of course the man was bestial to permit such a thing. But should he be the only one who goes to jail? Hadn't his wife also some responsibility? Was the third member of the card school – the wife's nineteen-year-old sister who seems to have been a constant sleeping partner of the husband's – entirely innocent?

The fourteen-year-old girl herself hardly sounds as if she will ever qualify to become a Methodist Sunday-school teacher.

Is the next man she seduces also going to be sent to jug?

I do not know. What I do know is that nothing will ever, ever persuade me to play rummy in Oldham.

Not even on a wet Sunday.

27 March 1977

◆━◆

The late Mr Matt Talbot, Dublin docker while he lived and currently a serious candidate for Roman Catholic saint-hood, must have been a remarkable man.

He was a lush, who, at the age of twenty-eight, suddenly one Saturday afternoon was converted in a Dublin bar. No one would lend him enough money to buy another drink.

He wandered outside and saw a dog sniffing at an empty bottle and in his mind the dog symbolized himself.

From that moment onwards not another drop crossed his lips.

He spent the rest of his life in prayer and devotion. When he died in 1925 it was discovered that he wore a hair shirt and heavy chains concealed under his clothes. It is now said that his life 'attained the peak of Christian perfection'.

But is it really the peak of Christian perfection to take to lemonade, put on a hair shirt and wear iron chains instead of braces?

If so, I tell you this, there are going to be damned few candidates for sainthood from Auchtermuchty.

10 April 1977

Dr Sam Oram, head of the Cardiac Unit at London's King's College Hospital, is clearly a superb doctor.

I know that from the flood of letters I received when I wrote some weeks ago about a colleague of mine who had undergone open-heart surgery at King's.

One reader is alive today because of the treatment he received at King's as long ago as 1963. He felt so conscious of the quality of the work being done in the Cardiac Unit that he wrote to three successive Prime Ministers, Tory and Socialist, suggesting that Dr Oram should be given a honour.

In each case, his suggestion was duly noted. Thirteen years later, Dr Oram has not had as much as a dicky-bird.

I wonder why.

Do you suppose that Dr Oram would still be a commoner if, instead of saving the lives of countless ordinary folk, he had clapped his stethoscope to Marcia's left breast?

26 September 1976

I stood barefoot on a thistle with my ironic remark the Sunday before Christmas that if chastity were to be the criterion for a lady being presented to Prince Charles, then who in the West End of London would he have to talk to save the Archbishop of Canterbury's wife?

By every post husbands have been indignantly assuring me that their own wives are every bit as chaste as Mrs Coggan.

I surrender. I accept without question the truth of what they say. Especially those who were kind enough to enclose pictures of their ladies.

2 January 1977

●●━━━●●

Tomorrow morning in the Royal Courts of Justice starts the curious case of Granada TV boss Lord Bernstein versus Ralph Ashley.

Who is Ralph Ashley? He is a man who runs a little aerial photography firm called Skyviews and General. He makes a living taking photographs of country houses from the air and then trying to sell the pictures to the house owners.

The Queen Mum and Old Gravel Voice himself have been among his satisfied customers.

But all hell was let loose when Mr Ashley's photographer flew over the 200-acre farm in Kent of Lord Bernstein.

His Lordship immediately issued a writ, alleging trespass of air space, invasion of privacy and 'anything else my lawyers can throw at them'.

Isn't that a hoot coming from a man whose company not so long ago sent a helicopter over Britain taking pictures of the rest of us without our permission?

Mr Ashley has offered to destroy the negative and promised not to photograph Lord Bernstein's house again. All to no avail.

So, for the 18 months the case has been pending, a small

businessman has lived in fear and trembling of what tomorrow will bring.

I have not the faintest idea if technically Lord Bernstein is right in his legal ownership of the air space above his house.

But I think it beneath contempt that any rich man should use his wealth and power in this vindictive fashion.

30 January 1977

●●━●●

Did you see that in Canada, a twenty-year-old girl had been ordered to give a pint of blood every 6 months for 2 years, after having admitted cheating on Social Security?

I tell you this. If they were to do the same thing here then there are some citizens who would be going round on their hands and knees suffering from chronic anaemia.

30 January 1977

●●━●●

I tell you a tale that ought to make your hair stand on end.

A young lady of my acquaintance, utterly respectable – in dress and appearance she could easily pass as a Sunday school teacher – entered a London Underground train at White City just before the evening rush hour at the same time as three coloured youths.

Two of them sat across the aisle opposite her, but the third, although there was a vacant seat beside his companions, choose to sit beside her. Soon she was aware that his elbow was pushing suggestively against her.

Not wishing to create a scene, she rose and went to the other end of the carriage.

Immediately all three youths started yelling: 'What's the

matter, lady? Don't you like black boys?'

There were perhaps a dozen white men in the carriage. Not one stirred.

The three youths pursued the girl the length of the carriage, surrounded her again, and one of them put his arm around her.

Terrified, she rose and sought sanctuary between two other women.

But her embarrassment did not end there. Before the youths left the train they confronted her menacingly and one of them said: 'Are you a racialist, lady? Don't you want to kiss a black backside?' Only backside was not the word he used.

What the hell are we coming to that we allow this sort of conduct to go on?

For ironically the only two people likely to be criticized for this incident are the girl, for having discriminated against the blacks, and me for having dared to write about it.

13 February 1977

•◄■►•

At breakfast in Edinburgh's North British Hotel, and in a dining room stuffed with tourists from every country in the world, the orange juice put in front of me tasted very much more of water than of orange.

I asked the head waiter if it was just possible that it had been watered.

He whisked my glass away and returned with one which really contained orange juice.

'How could it happen,' I asked, 'that water got into the orange juice?'

He smiled. 'You know what boys are like,' he replied.

Of course I know what boys are like. But if in a British Rail hotel as big as the North British in Edinburgh the orange juice is being watered, then what in God's name do you suppose they are doing to the whisky?

Nice isn't it, to come back from holiday and find a quarrel with an old friend settled?

On 16 May last year I published in this column an item which caused the Rt Hon. Sir James Harold Wilson to blow a gasket.

In it I wondered aloud why Sir Harold seemed so obsessed with the idea that the scandal then surrounding Mr Jeremy Thorpe might be the work of South African agents.

By hot hand came a letter from Sir Harold's solicitors, describing the item as 'grossly defamatory of our client' and demanding an unreserved apology and statement in open court; the removal of the libel from all back numbers of the *Sunday Express* in our possession and indeed from all back numbers in public libraries.

I am happy to report that the matter between Sir Harold and myself has now been settled.

Has there been a statement in open court? No. Has the item had been removed from all back numbers? No.

Instead, Sir Harold has taken out of court a sum of money in full settlement for the defamation of his good name.

How much was his good name worth? £105.

Isn't it lucky I didn't libel Marcia too? It might have cost another fiver.

28 August 1977

When I saw on TV the brave little children honoured at No. 10 Downing Street last week, the one who brought a lump to my throat was little Kirk Peters, a spina bifida victim who has spent much of his nine years in hospital, who can barely move his head, and yet still had in his cheerful, happy, mischievous little face all the courage in the world.

Please God, may Kirk and all other children like him have as happy a Christmas as, with their shining eyes and trusting faith, they give to those who love them.

21 December 1980

The Prince of Wales put on a sizzling turn of speed when he steamed away from twenty-two-year-old Australian model Miss Bree Summers on Bondi beach.

With that sort of acceleration, the next time he turns out at Sandown Park, might he not avoid doing damage to the little finger of his left hand if he took the jumps without the horse?

Come to that, and always provided he is being chased by a twenty-two-year-old model, might he not be faster too?

19 April 1981

Have you ever reflected on just how tough a life the Queen has?

For the last 27 years she has had to stand back and watch this country dwindle from a world Power into an assembly plant for Japanese cars.

At State Openings of Parliament she has had to read out platitudinous speeches written for her by Ministers, many of whom were not fit to lick her boots, and often containing political programmes destined to kick Britain further down the road to ruin.

Yet in no way has she ever been able to give even the slightest hint of how or what she personally feels.

Any more than she will be able to during the election campaign that has now started.

It may be she thinks Mr Callaghan is the greatest thing since Harry Lauder, it may even be that she cannot stand the smell of Mrs Thatcher's perfume.

But by not one flicker of an eyelash can she publicly show her emotions.

While all the rest of us can take an active part in the fight and can by our vote decide this country's future, she can do nothing except acquiescently await the will and wisdom of the people.

Would you really be surprised if sometimes she feels like jacking it all in?

8 April 1979

··──··

It is enormously sad that a seventeen-year-old Turkish-Cypriot girl should have jumped to her death from the balcony of her family home in East London rather than face up to being questioned by her parents about whether she had lost her virginity.

But isn't it almost equally sad that in the average British family it would not be the seventeen-year-old girl who would be scared of answering the question but the parents who would be far too terrified even to ask it?

22 April 1979

••—••

Late on the Saturday night of Orthodox Easter, there was a glittering and almost unprecedented attraction for the glamour-starved young on Russian TV — a special disco programme featuring Abba and packed full of gorgeous girls in scanty clothing.

It was, of course, an attempt to keep the young Russians away from the churches.

The attempt failed. As always at Easter the churches throughout Russia were crammed.

In life there are not many things of which I am certain. But of this I am sure.

No matter how long it takes. No matter what hardships still be in store. In the end in Russia it is the Church not Communism that will prevail.

29 April 1979

••—••

The political career of Lord George-Brown has been marvellous.

There was the hilarious occasion — maybe apocryphal but I would like to think true — when as Foreign Secretary and full of the best of spirits, he attended some splendid formal reception at the Peruvian Embassy. The band struck up and he approached a person magnificently attired in scarlet robes and said: 'Would you care to dance with me?'

And received the frosty reply: 'No thanks. That's the Peruvian national anthem and I am the papal legate.'

There was the sadder time when he was photographed lying on the pavement outside the Palace of Westminster.

Now Lord George-Brown announces his intention to

re-enter politics – this time as a candidate for Derbyshire in the European Parliament.

What do I say? Just this. If I lived in Derbyshire I would unhesitatingly vote for him.

He is a better patriot and a more honest man than all the rest of the Labour Party put together.

And a damned sight better than the vast majority of the Tory Party, too.

I hope that he will give us his counsel for a long, long time.

28 May 1978

∎—∎

The photograph of strikers' leader Leszek Walesa bowing before Roman Catholic Bishop Henryk Jankowski after attending Mass at the Lenin shipyard in Gdansk symbolizes for me the ferment in Poland.

It was Stalin who once sneered: 'How many divisions has the Pope?'

In Poland Stalin's successor Comrade Brezhnev now knows.

Nor is it only Poland. In Rumania, in Hungary, throughout Eastern Europe, the religious tinders are ready to be set aflame. Nor will Russia herself be safe.

For long the crowded congregations at Orthodox churches have been worrying Communist authorities. So has the craze of young Russians for wearing gold crosses round their necks and Jesus T-Shirts.

A letter in *Pravda* from a party member told how shocked he was at seeing a cross 'not on the neck of an old woman, but on the chests of sturdy fellows, striding along the beaches of the Black sea'.

I have said it before, and I will say it again.

There are few things in life of which I am sure, but of one thing I am quite certain.

Long after Communism has been dead and buried in Russia and throughout Eastern Europe, Christianity will be alive and kicking.

31 August 1980

In an interview in *Financial Weekly* Mr Moss Evans, General Secretary of the TGWU, says: 'Where many people misunderstand British workers is that they have not got the same philosophy as workers in the United States or Germany. They do not want to be millionaires. They just want a decent standard of living.'

Do not want to be millionaires?

What then does Mr Evans suppose all that scratching of pens is about every Thursday night?

Ten million British workers writing home to Mum? Or ten million British workers filling in their football pools?

22 April 1979

Mr Raymond Andrews, the senior partner in a firm of architects, thought it would be a good idea to fly the Union Jack from the top of the main boiler chimney of a housing project his firm had designed for the Notting Hill Housing Trust. But after a few days the flag had to be taken down because if offended the coloured people in the district who thought it represented the National Front.

Isn't it a mercy Mr Andrews didn't start a real riot by having a band play God Save the Queen?

29 April 1979

<hr />

That Anna Ford should turn down a £75,000 offer from Mr Paul Raymond to model nude does not surprise me.

Miss Ford is not only a lovely lady. She also has a good, sensible mind between her pretty ears.

What does stagger me is the insight the incident has given us into the economics of female nudity.

£75,000 for Miss Ford?

What, then, in heaven's name do you suppose they would pay for Marcia?

It is, of course, a sad reflection on our prurient society.

But isn't it also a mite unfair that while famous ladies will know from now on that they are sitting on gold mines there is little in it for famous men?

Can you imagine anyone offering more than 5p for a full frontal of Ted Heath or Harold Wilson?

3 June 1979

<hr />

The IRA terrorist who carefully affixed Irish stamps to the letter bombs he posted in Birmingham is never likely to come among the top ten in even a Brain of Ireland contest.

But at least it means that it shouldn't really take a Sherlock Holmes to find him.

With his IQ, isn't he quite likely to be found in the queue at an automatic car wash – sitting astride a motor-bike?

17 June 1979

··————··

There was nothing much wrong with forty-nine-year-old Mr Patrick McCann.

But because his laboratory reports at Walsgrave Hospital, Coventry, got mixed up with another patient's he was operated on for cancer. And died.

The hospital says it was a chance in a million.

And maybe it was.

All I know is that I would think twice before going to Walsgrave Hospital to have my tonsils removed. I would not wish to run the risk of ending up singing soprano.

18 November 1979

··————··

In the evening newspapers of last Wednesday there was a happy picture and story of thirteen Spiller's flour mill workers who shared a win of £750,085.95 on the pools.

Everyone knows their names and everyone knows exactly how much each received – £57,698.91.

On the same night in Glasgow, a man, woman or maybe even a child learned that he or she had won £250,000 in the September draw for Premium Bonds. Unless he or she chooses to tell us, the lucky winner will remain unknown for all time.

Nor will we know the name of whoever won £100,000 in yesterday's draw.

Aren't we carrying the secrecy concerning the winners of Premium Bonds just a bit too far?

We take for granted that the draw is honest, the administrators incorruptible, the winners genuine, and that there is not even the slightest sniff of a fiddle.

But have you ever personally met anyone or even heard of anyone who has won a prize any bigger than £1,000?

Wouldn't it be nice to know for sure that larger prize winners do in fact exist?

7 September 1980

‣——‣

It has been a remarkable story, the realization of the dream of fifty-eight-year-old Edward McGlynn.

For 40 years, he has been unable to work.

But throughout all these years, subsisting entirely on a disability pension and state handouts, Mr McGlynn has had one ambition. That his son Adrian would go to Eton.

For the last 11 years every spare penny has gone into educational insurance policies. Every year the premiums have risen. They are now £96 a month. But they have been and are being paid.

And Adrian, now thirteen years old, will soon be going to his posh school.

I have no wish to detract from this wonderful tale of a father's touching devotion to his son.

Nor to underestimate the sacrifices he and his wife have made.

But is it not slightly ironic that on state handouts alone Mr McGlynn has been able to achieve what is quite beyond the financial capacity of many a managing director?

2 December 1979

It was a splendid idea of the Tory-controlled Edinburgh Council to present Jack Nicklaus with a silver putter.

But ever since the decision was taken, Scotland has been rocked by the story of how the putter came to be placed in Mr Nicklaus's hand.

Not one but four council officials, headed by the Lord Provost, flew the Atlantic to the Ohio Open in May to present it. Not only at ratepayers expense. Not only first class. But – just to show that expense didn't matter – by Concorde.

Isn't it enough to make you weep – especially when just 8 weeks later Mr Nicklaus was coming to Edinburgh anyway to play in the British Open at Muirfield and was to be guest of honour at a civic reception?

When their snouts are in the trough, isn't it extraordinary how difficult it is from a rear view to tell a Socialist pig from a Tory pig?

3 August 1980

Can it really be possible, as reported in the High Court, that at a dinner the Chairman of the Football Association, Sir Harold Thompson, turned to the England manager,

Don Revie, and said: 'When I get to know you better Revie, I will call you Don.'?

If it is a matter of surprise that a nasty money grubber like Mr Revie should ever have become manager of England, is it not equally surprising that a pompous twit like Sir Harold Thompson should ever have become Chairman of the FA?

2 December 1979

I read with incredulity that because she did not wear a bra, a beautiful German girl translating for a high-ranking officer, Brigadier-General David C. Martin, at the Mainz Asparagus Festival, had been sacked.

Sacked for not wearing a bra?

What can have come over the US Army?

Are these really the same sort of chaps who once upon a time chased everything in skirts – with the possible exception of the Highland Light Infantry?

Besides, how did the General know what the lass was wearing?

Shouldn't he have been keeping his eyes on his notes and his mind on the asparagus?

4 June 1978

᠁᠁

Abandoned baby Nicola Michelle would probably not even be alive if twenty-nine-year-old Police Constable Michael Barker had not found her in a yellow plastic bag in Ormiston Park, Derby.

Every day thereafter Police Constable Barker and his wife visited her in Derby City Hospital.

The Barkers have already two sons of their own. But they wanted to adopt Nicola Michelle.

Isn't it almost unbelievable that their application has been turned down on the ground that Police Constable Barker was 'too emotionally involved'?

Would he have stood a better chance if he hadn't given a damn about the child?

26 September 1980

᠁᠁

Tomorrow night in Manchester Town Hall, the staff of the City's Housing Department gather for the Christmas beano.

Nothing elaborate of course, just a simple little buffet of chicken legs, sandwiches, cakes and trifles.

To drink there will be whisky, gin, wine, and beer; sweet sherry for the ladies; fruit juices for the teetotallers.

All, of course, paid for by the ratepayers.

Anything else to report?

Just that any city councillors who attend will be able to

claim an allowance of £8 if they stay drinking for less than 3 hours, £12.14 if they are there for more than 3 hours, and if by chance they should still be holding on to a whisky glass after 4 hours, they may claim £15.27 – plus travelling expenses.

Wonderful old life, isn't it – for councillors?

9 December 1979

It must have been fascinating, that mid air near-mutiny on the shuttle flight between Washington and New York when Mr Richard Lent, a non-smoking lawyer, was unable to get a seat in the plane's non-smoking section and insisted that passengers around him in the smoking section should stub out their fags.

Moreover, he was, under American aviation rules, within his rights.

In their wrath, the smokers stood up and told Mr Lent what they thought about him. So fiercely that the plane had to be landed.

On whose side am I? Without a shadow of doubt, the smokers'.

Mr Lent, like so many who share his obsessional opposition to smoking, sounds a proper prune.

For my own part when I travel either by air or train I invariably choose the smoking section. Not because I necessarily want to smoke myself. But because in smoking sections you always meet a better and more tolerant class of person. More attractive birds, too.

9 December 1979

My sympathy is entirely with businessman Tom Granby who agreed to sponsor a charity swim by a Bunny Girl at a rate of £2.50 for every length of the pool she completed.

He expected, on information supplied by the girl herself, to have to pay out a total of, at the very outside, £50. A generous enough contribution.

What he did not know was that she was a marathon swimmer. She completed 1,214 lengths and Mr Granby is now being pressed to pay £3,000 to the handicapped children's unit at Charing Cross Hospital, London.

He is refusing to do so. And good as the cause is, I back him in that refusal.

There are times when charity demands come perilously close to moral blackmail. And this is one of them.

16 December 1979

***

Isn't it a hoot that in the Dining Club reserved for senior staff at London Transport every meal provided costs the tax-payer between £20 and £30 a time – and that fifteen of the most senior officers have Daimler Sovereigns, Jaguars, and Rovers and chauffeurs at their personal disposal?

Do you suppose that any of them has actually ever been inside a bus or tube except when accompanying royalty at the opening of a new line?

And isn't it almost unbelievable that this should be going on in a disastrously incompetent enterprise which, even with subsidies of £130 million, is still losing a further £10 million a year?

23 December 1979

***

It is sad that the lemon is not after all going to be a great source of energy – although it has been proved that the acid in one single fruit is enough to power a digital clock.

But isn't even that marvellous? And doesn't it open up

some wonderful prospects?

Aren't there in your neck of the woods, as there certainly are in mine, sharp-tongued ladies who, if properly plugged in, could produce enough acid to keep Big Ben going for a month?

No, no, please God, I don't mean you Alice.

6 January 1980

It is understandable if, when a goalkeeper and a centreforward go up for a ball together, the centre-forward's elbow accidentally brushes the goalkeeper's face.

But when, as a result the goalkeeper has two teeth rammed to the back of his mouth and his upper jaw broken, as happened to Tottenham Hotspur goalkeeper Milija Aleksic, can it still be termed an accident?

Spurs manager Mr Keith Burkinshaw says yes and exonerates Manchester United striker, Joe Jordan.

And, of course, I accept that verdict.

But if that is indeed the way Mr Jordan accidentally moves his elbow, then all I can say is that I hope to God I never find myself in the same queue as him for the last bus home.

13 January 1980

It is said that the average Chinese peasant now has in his bank a total of £2.85.

Poor so-and-so's.

I know exactly how they feel.

Do you suppose that the cost of gas, electricity, mortages, TV licences, train travel, and booze have all gone up at the same time there too?

20 January 1980

One of the very few disadvantages of being a top politician is, I suppose, the fact that you can hardly spend Thursday evenings filling in football coupons.

Still, why bother with the Treble Chance, when you can become rich simply by writing your memoirs?

Sir Harold Wilson must have at least £300,000 of publisher's money in the bank, building society, or just tucked under the mattress.

The late Richard Crossman can hardly have made less than £200,000 from his diaries.

We have been told that the fee for Mr Callaghan's story is likely to be at least £250,000.

Now even a political minnow like Mrs Barbara Castle is trilling happily on her way to the bank with £30,000 crammed into a holdall.

Good luck to them all. I grudge these great Socialist egalitarians not a penny.

But couldn't we at least be told how much, if anything, they either have paid or are going to pay in tax?

20 January 1980

•••—•••

Isn't it astounding that in the 500-year history of Eton its new headmaster, Mr Eric Anderson, should be the very first Scot to get the job?

How in God's name can the school have managed to survive for so long?

But do you wonder why, in these circumstances, so many Old Etonians who become Guards officers and Cabinet Ministers couldn't even tell what day of the week it was without a competent NCO or Civil Servant to advise them?

27 January 1980

•••—•••

In his shoddy little story about his brother Roddy's love affair with Princess Margaret, that nasty little creep, Mr Dai Llewellyn, takes a passing swipe at Bianca Jagger. He sneers that Bianca's mother used to have a Coca-Cola stand in Nicaragua.

So what?

Isn't selling Coca-Cola a damned sight more honourable than shopping your brother and his lover for £30,000?

27 January 1980

***

As he lay on the ground Mr Anthony Blunt's homosexual friend William Gaskin explained how during the middle of the night he had come to fall 80 feet from a balcony of the flat they share in London.

'I was looking for a breath of fresh air,' he gasped.

With a skunk like Blunt still inside the flat, do you wonder?

17 February 1980

***

I take this quote from a diocesan letter of the Bishop of Lincoln:

'Some will see Scripture and the Church's tradition as allowing only self-restraint as a possible moral option for homosexual people. Others, and I am one of them, while taking seriously what Scripture and tradition seem to say, think it necessary also to take seriously the manifest fact of those tender serious, faithful and creative relationships which homosexual men and women sometimes establish, in which genital acts clearly contribute to the tenderness.'

It is these characteristics I would always look for in a

relationship. When I find them I cannot say that such a relationship is contrary to the will of God.'

Would you care to read that again?

In which genital acts clearly contribute to the tenderness!

It is almost unbelievable that such words could come from a bishop.

Is our new Archbishop of Canterbury going to tell us without equivocation whether or not he agrees with Lincoln?

2 March 1980

That there should now be more marriageable men than women is a matter for rejoicing.

It has always seemed to me monstrously unfair that because of the preponderance of females women have had

to wait, often in increasing desperation, for a man to do the chasing.

But now the boot is on the other foot, will it be the lassies who in future make the advances?

Could the day yet come when a fellow will have to think twice and tighten his sporran before accepting a lift from a car driven by a lassie?

It is a prospect that may strike terror into the hearts of Englishmen. But I tell you this, if and when that day should really arrive, there are some chaps in Auchtermuchty who are going to spend their holidays hitch-hiking.

9 July 1978

In her short life there was not much going for four-year-old Mandy McGibbon.

She spent 18 days in hospital suffering from 'non-accidental' injuries – like being branded with an electric iron and immersed in a bath of cold water.

When she returned home, her step-father, twenty-year-old Robert Granger killed her by punching her in the stomach.

For that he was sent to a young offenders' institution for 6 years.

Only 6 years? Wouldn't sixty, plus sixty punches in the stomach have been more appropriate?

2 March 1980

The action of twenty-year-old Private Cheryl Taylor of the US Seventh Army in grabbing nineteen-year-old Trooper Kevin Knox by his private parts and saying: 'Give me a light, you shrimp,' was that of a very forward hussy.

And Trooper Knox was within his rights in charging her

with assault and battery.

Nor do I complain about the fine of £150 and 30 days hard labour imposed on Miss Taylor.

But isn't it all a sad reflection on the way the US Army has changed?

Do you remember the good old days when it was the lassies not the laddies who screamed for help?

13 April 1980

The letter from D.T. Shah, of Edgware, Middlesex stood out like a dirty thumb among the applications for the job of dispensing optician advertised by the firm of C.W. Dixey & Son Ltd, Wigmore Street, London.

It was written on a tatty piece of paper from a looseleaf notebook. In its few brief lines it contained two spelling errors. He even got the name of the firm wrong.

Since the job required the highest standards of accuracy, a polite letter was written to Mr Shah telling him, quite truthfully as it happened, that the post had been filled.

End of story? Like Hell.

The firm has now received twelve pages of bumph from a complaints officer of the Commission for Racial Equality containing a questionnaire demanding to know, among other things, why Mr Shah was not given an interview; the ethnic origins of the candidates who were interviewed, including the one who got the job.

As it happens the firm of C.W. Dixey has an excellent record in race relations. Two out of its fourteen dispensing opticians are Indians.

But is it not in itself discriminatory that although an Englishman can be rejected at will, a firm cannot turn down a coloured applicant, no matter how unsuitable, without being asked in intimidatory fashion to explain why?

And asked by whom?

The name of the complaints officer who wrote to C.W. Dixey was a Mr Ameer Ali – from which I would deduce that he does not play the harp and does not come from Aberdovey.

When I rang the commission and asked to speak to Mr Ali. I was asked by a lady with a sing-song voice: 'Which Mr Ali do you want?' I have since learned that out of the commission's staff of 229, no less than 55 per cent are non-whites.

Aren't there times when you trully feel like pulling the duvet over your head and turning your face towards the wall?

14 September 1980

11—11

At an age when some contemporaries, who have led lives much more chaste and much more pure, get puffed playing dominoes, Frank Sinatra again takes London by storm.

The Festival Hall is crammed with people young and old, eager to hear him sing.

And all the old magic is still there.

I know it will upset my former members of the Band of Hope. But isn't his achievement a wonderful advertisement for a life-long diet of birds and booze?

Pass the Glen Grant please, Selina.

10 September 1980

11—11

He is just five years old and in court he was referred to only as Robert.

He was born prematurely at 28 weeks. From the beginning it was touch and go.

His heart stopped several times. He needed 100 per cent

oxygen. As a result of that oxygen, perhaps over too long a period, his eyes were affected and he was permanently blinded.

Now through his guardians he is suing London's Westminster Hospital for negligence.

Who are his guardians?

Westminster City Council. For Robert is now in the council's care awaiting adoption.

Poor little mite.

Even if he were awarded all the money in the world will it ever mean as much to this little unwanted blind boy as would his mother's loving arms around him?

16 March 1980

Mr Prasanta Mukherjee has cost us £72,000 in helicopters, aircraft and warships searching the Channel.

Even so, I find it difficult to have anything except admiration for a chap who buys for £1,700 a rotten hulk, loads it

'up with curry and porridge and sets off for Calcutta with such guts and in such ignorance that he has to ask a police launch which way to turn when he reaches the Isle of Wight.

Besides, isn't it a damn sight better to have an Asian in his own boat asking the way home, rather than one arriving at London Airport asking the way to the nearest Social Security office?

10 July 1977

••➤••

When that Saudi Arabian prince ordered the execution of his own granddaughter for adultery, it would be racially arrogant to suppose that he did so with anything other than a heavy heart.

Love for one's children and grandchildren is not an Anglo-Saxon prerogative.

So while I defend the right of Lord Grade's ATV to make *Death of a Princess*, I can understand Saudi Arabian anger at what they thought was a deliberate attack on their religious beliefs. I can even understand their quite wrongly-based suspicion that the programme was actuated by a Jewish dislike of everything Arab.

What I completely fail to understand is the onslaught on Lord Carrington because he expressed 'profound regret' at the offence the programme might have caused to Islamic law and religion.

What did we expect him to do? Spit in the eye of a nation whose business contracts with this country run into hundreds of millions of pounds?

Instead of criticizing either Lord Carrington or Saudi Arabia, shouldn't we just be thankful that the same harsh law concerning adultery does not apply here?

For if it did, I can tell you that in my neck of the woods and maybe in Lord Grade's too, there would not be enough people left alive to make up a four at bridge.

13 April 1980

••➤••

In advertisements arrestingly headed, 'Stop Janice walking the streets. Give her a home now', London's Westminster City Council is seeking foster parents for teenage girls who have been taken into care.

But it is what they are offering foster parents that makes me whistle. £35 a week for board and lodging. Plus a further payment of £50 a week, tax free, 85 quid a week in all. And even that is much less than half the cost of keeping the same girl in a council home.

Aren't we off our tiny little nuts when for one delinquent teenage girl, ratepayers have to provide more money than most of those ratepayers themselves have to bring up a whole family?

5 October 1980

⁘⁘⁘

Muhammad Ali tells of how, during his visit to London, two beautiful nineteen-year-old girls, one white, one coloured, knocked on the door of his hotel room, asked for his autograph, and then suggested that they might come in and stay a little while.

Said Ali: 'Any man would have desired them, but I said to myself . . . here comes the devil. So I gave them the autograph and sent them away. God was testing me.'

It is marvellous that Muhammad Ali withstood temptation. And quite natural that after such a struggle, he was rather less than his usual articulate self when the next day he had to record Desert Island Discs for the BBC.

Had the same thing happened to a member of the Auchtermuchty curling club, it is more than possible that after wrestling with the devil all night, the following morning he would hardly have been able to get up off his knees to put on his kilt.

21 December 1980

⁘⁘⁘

There are just forty names on the crumbling war memorial in the village of Grimston, Norfolk. Forty young men who died in two World Wars.

It would cost £2,500 to put it right. But since the money is not available the memorial is to be demolished.

There are 1,800 villagers in Grimston.

I wish them luck as they down their pints, fill in their football pools, and study next year's holiday brochures.

Better luck than those forty young men had so long ago.

5 October 1980

At the end of their onesided battle for the heavy-weight championship of the world, Larry Holmes went to the corner of the defeated, dejected Muhammad Ali and whispered in his ear: 'I love you, man. I respect you. You're my brother. Any time you need me I'll be there.'

His action and his words caused me to reflect, not for the first time, that professional boxing might be a more acceptable sport if only some of the middle-aged fur-coated women who sit at the ringside baying for blood and some of the yobboes who throw empty beer cans filled with urine were one tenth as decent as the men who do the fighting.

5 October 1980

Sandy Lyle ended the golf season as Number One in Europe with earnings of over £43,000 and that is only the tip of the iceberg. I estimate that he must have made over £100,000 already this year — and all this at the age of just twenty-two.

Yet he is completely unspoilt. I played golf with him last Monday and in atrocious weather conditions he lugged his own bag round the course.

I also chanced to see his passport. It was issued before he

reached his present dizzy heights but it says a great deal of the modesty of this likeable young man. In the space where he describes his occupation, that occupation still reads 'Assistant Greenkeeper'.

12 October 1980

The Pope's pronouncement that a man is guilty of 'adultery in the heart' if he looks with lust at his own wife may have produced consternation in Rome.

In Auchtermuchty, it can only have produced a lifting of the heart in many a laddie who suddenly realized that by these terms of reference he had been sinless for years.

May I point out to such poor deluded fools that His Holiness's edict applies to the wives of other men too?

19 October 1980

The blackboard sign put up by Mrs Barbara Blanchard outside her Scunthorpe corner grocer's shop seemed innocent enough. 'We serve you the good old British way. Try it for a change.'

Isn't it marvellous that because there is an Asian grocer's across the way she should be told by an officer from the local Community Relations Council, a Mrs Rashmi Malik, that the word British was offensive and that unless she changed it she could be in breach of the racial discrimination laws?

Or should we just thank God that, at least for the moment, we are still allowed to call Sir Peter Parker's chuff-chuffs, British Rail?

26 October 1980

As I watched Mr Michael Foot on TV the other night I remembered the first time I saw that stick on which he leaned.

It was 1964. I had gone to visit Lord Beaverbrook in the South of France. Mr Foot, then painfully recovering from the car crash with caused his present limp, was already there as a house guest.

It was clear that Beaverbrook was dying. And that the end could come suddenly. I wanted an obituary of him ready to be published in the *Sunday Express*. Michael Foot, as a long-time associate of Beaverbrook was clearly the best man to do it.

He and I walked along the cliff edge at Cap D'Ail. I asked him if he was prepared to take on the task. I promised him that if he did so no one would know about it until Lord Beaverbrook died. I offered him a considerable amount of money.

I still remember how Michael Foot ground the ferrule of his walking stick into the turf of the cliff top. Then he said: 'No, I cannot, I love that old man and I would not want to write anything which might mean I wished to hasten his death.'

I do not know many good things about Michael Foot. But at least a chap cannot be all bad who is loyal to the man who has been his boss.

2 November 1980

The look on the face of the guard of the London to Glasgow express, thirty-four-year-old Mr Thomas McCondochie, must have been quite something when having stopped his train by emergency brakes he walked along the line to the driving cab and found it empty.

The driver, forty-two-year-old Hugh Harvey, was 4 miles

back along the line, flat on his face on the embankment and with an alcoholic blood count of 174.

Presumably he had turned left instead of right when leaving his cab in search of the first-class loo. Lucky he didn't try to light a fag on the way. He might have blown the whole train up.

Unhappily Mr Harvey is not unique among engine drivers. In 4 years 800 railwaymen have appeared before disciplinary hearings for drunkenness.

Yet last week the NUR conference was urging greater understanding and no sacking for railwaymen who drink!

Greater understanding my foot. I would have random breath tests with instant dismissal for those who offend.

Or would that provoke a national rail strike? With Mr Arthur Scargill organizing the pickets around Euston Station?

17 July 1977

Mr Brian Clough tells us that he is going to think over the prospect of becoming a Socialist MP.

Would he make a good one?

I have to admit he has a lot going for him.

He is a big head with not too much between his ears, arrogant beyond measure and never stops talking.

But doesn't Mr Clough realize that with these qualities he is unique in football, whereas if ever he went to Westminster the only way he could distinguish himself from his fellow Socialist MPs would be by the colour of his braces?

16 November 1980

 ◆━◆

At the age of forty-five and if her photographs do her justice, not everyone's idea of a raving beauty, divorcee, Mrs Roberta Parkes, seems to have a way with lodgers.

She has just been to High Court in order to stop one of them, Mr Ian White-Smith, handsome and 10 years her junior from pestering her with his attentions.

Besotted with love he is said to have telephoned Mrs Parkes eight times a day.

Nor is Mrs Parkes now alone. She was accompanied to court by a new lodger whom she describes as 'super' and says that he Hoovers his room, launders his own sheets, cleans the bath and walks the dog.

With lodgers like these and with hundreds of thousands of middle-aged ladies eager to share her secret doesn't Mrs Parkes realize that she must be sitting on a fortune?

What in Heaven's name can she be sprinkling on the All-bran?

2 November 1980

 ◆━◆

Mr Harry Slatter, caretaker of a Tottenham, London, school, tells us that his wages are his own business.

Are they really? Are they not everyone's business when he is getting £14,168 a year, plus an index-linked pension, plus free gas, electricity, telephone and virtually free accommodation?

Nor is Mr Slatter alone among his kind in enjoying the lush life.

In the Socialist-controlled London Borough of Harringay alone there are eleven school caretakers earning more than £10,000 a year.

And the plaintive, and I suspect truthful, cry which goes up is that they are simply trying to catch up with plumbers and dustmen.

What in God's name, then can the Harringay plumbers and dustmen be earning?

And isn't it marvellous that many of the latter will soon be rattling their collecting boxes under the noses of old age pensioners?

23 November 1980

⊷

In Matthew Moss Middle School, Rochdale, where 84 per cent of the 600 pupils are English, the parents of some eighty Asian children did not wish them to attend morning assembly because it included Christian prayers.

Now because the headmaster, Mr A.H. Fletcher, does not wish to offend or isolate the Asian children, all Christian worship in the school has been suspended altogether.

Isn't that incredible?

Or are we supposed to be thankful that the tolerant, broadminded Mr Fletcher, has at least stopped short of ordering all 600 to get down on their knees five times a day and turn their tiny faces towards Mecca?

30 November 1980

I looked outside my bedroom window shortly after 7 o'clock the other morning and there, less than 40 feet from the house, were three deer eating the last of the windfalls from under an apple tree.

It was a moment of magic less than 30 miles from London.

I watched entranced for perhaps 3 minutes. A jet flew overhead. The ears of the deer pricked. Then relaxed.

A lorry rattled noisily past in a nearby lane. Again the ears pricked and the deer stood tense for perhaps 15 seconds. Then back to the apples.

But the very second that hopeful camera in hand, I undid the catch on my window they were lolloping off like the wind.

A sad comment on our species, isn't it, when wild animals can become accustomed to strange modern noises they know are of no danger to them and yet are immediately alert when a sudden click warns them of a man who might have in his hands not a camera but a gun?

30 November 1980

━━━

In Natal, there is a move afoot to end the system set up whereby, in an effort to stop the growing trend towards Western permissiveness, young Zulu maidens are subjected to compulsory 'virginity tests'.

Any girl who refuses to take the test is fined about £20 – twice as much as if she takes the test and fails it.

As for the man who has deflowered the maiden, if he is traced he has to give two head of cattle to the girl's parents.

Critics of the virginity test are now complaining it is all highly unethical and costing humble people too much money.

I can understand how they feel.

If they had similar tests in Scotland there are some

farmers I know not too far from Auchtermuchty who would never again have to get up early.

For in their byres, poor laddies, there wouldn't be a single cow left to milk.

29 July 1979

◗◖◀◗◖

It is being said that while he was a student at Keele University, the Rt Hon. Anthony Wedgwood Benn's eldest son Stephen, aged twenty-nine, was forced to live in poverty, since his parents' wealth precluded his being given a grant and his own independent nature prevented his accepting money from his father and mother.

We are told he was so hard up that he could not afford to pay for his digs and that at night he used to bed down under a desk in an office building.

Isn't that an extraordinary story?

His grandmother on his mother's side left something like £300,000 in 1974 on trust for her daughter's four children. His father's family is, at least by my standards, stinking rich too.

Did neither Anthony Wedgwood Benn nor his wife know of the conditions in which their son was living? Had Stephen no access to the trust fund which by now must have grown enormously in value? Or could the story about his poverty at Keele have anything to do with the fact that he has been adopted as Socialist candidate for a seat in the Greater London Council elections?

And by the time he becomes a Parliamentary candidate will we be told how, as a child, he used to go hungry and barefoot to council school?

Pass the sick bag Alice.

26 December 1980

There were ten crackers in the box I paid £1.95 for in W.H. Smith.

On Christmas Day eight out of the ten failed to make even the slightest little pop.

It would be nice to think that I was the only one in Britain who got a dud box. And that the one disappointed little face at my table was not mirrored ten-thousand-fold throughout the land by children not yet old enough to understand that for some people Christmas is just another day on which to make a quick profit.

28 December 1980

In the Roman Catholic Archdiocese of St Andrews and Edinburgh, Cardinal Gray is insisting that in future couples wishing to marry must give 6 months' notice before they can do so in church.

I can understand the cardinal's reasoning. He wants to reduce marriage breakdowns to a minimum.

But in that hot-blooded impetuous land of swinging

sporrans from which I hail, isn't His Eminence running a terrible risk of having to have wedding and christening services on the very same day?

29 December 1980

॥━॥

We learn that Lord Cowdrey one of the richest men in Britain, uses a senior citizen's rail card when he travels and that recently he has been journeying from his 50,000-acre estate in Scotland to his 17,000-acre Cowdray Park in Sussex for a token fare of £1. In a second class compartment presumably.

And then jumping into his chauffeured Rolls-Royce for the final few miles to his mansion.

How's that for canniness in a laddie who has to be worth £100 million?

Do you know something? I suspect that if like me he were mean enough to buy Christmas crackers at £1.95 a box, every single one of his would go pop.

4 January 1981

॥━॥

To all those suffering from post-Hogmanay depression, I offer this cheering January thought.

Isn't it marvellous to be able to watch the snowdrops grow, rather than be under them?

4 January 1981

॥━॥

Spurred on by the fact that Mr Kevin Keegan, no doubt for a huge fee, was promoting the project, the 150 children of Waverley Junior School in Crowthorne, in common with children at 3,000 other schools throughout the country, ate their way through mountains of baked beans in order to secure sports equipment for their school.

They managed to collect 2,000 labels – only to discover

to their bitter disappointment that they were 1,500 labels short of the number required for even a new match foot-ball.

Three thousand five hundred cans of beans for a football?

Isn't it a mercy for 150 little tummies, not to mention the Clean Air Society, that they hadn't set their sights on a swimming pool?

25 January 1981

–––

I have never thought that a gentleman who wears a vest and long-johns would ever be likely to be caught doing the carioca with Raquel Welch.

Nor that a lady who wears black suspender belts would have aspirations to become a Mother Superior.

So I agree with Sheffield Polytechnic lecturer Mrs Patricia Waring when she tells us that 'Clothes convey information about personality and attitudes such as aggression, rebellion and sexual availability.'

But can she really mean it when she adds that by wearing a scarf a man may be subconsciously indicating that he is starved of affection?

And if so could she explain why many a kilted Auchtermuchty laddie with a thick, long, warm scarf round his neck, still has modestly to cross his legs every time he sits down in public?

Hasn't it occurred to Mrs Waring that he might just possibly, and hopefully, be planning to use it as a ground sheet?

11 January 1981

–––

From the Old Bailey trial we learn that five out of the six terrorists who took over the Iranian Embassy in Princes

Gate deliberately chose death because they believed that to die in a just cause is a direct path to paradise.

The sixth terrorist, twenty-three-year-old Fowzi Nejad, apparently did not share the view of the other five. When the SAS stormed the embassy he lay down with the women hostages and pretended to be one of them.

Isn't that instinct for self-preservation uncannily reminiscent of another and more familiar group of contemporary terrorists?

Could it just be possible that Mr Nejad's mother came from Ireland?

25 January 1981

The whole world knows why Prince Charles went to Switzerland. To ski.

Yet the Court Circular, 23 January, solemnly announced: 'The Prince of Wales, attended by the Hon. Edward Adeane, left Royal Air Force Marham this morning in an aircraft of the Queen's Flight to visit the Federal Institute of Technology in Zurich.'

And it is true that the Prince did briefly visit the Institute on his way to the ski slopes.

Just as in 1979 he blessed with his fleeting presence a yoghurt factory and in 1980 the British Chamber of Commerce in Zurich.

What is it all about? Is the Prince fearful that unless he has the excuse of a duty visit to Switzerland, there would be criticism of his using an official aircraft purely for private pleasure?

If so, I would counsel the Prince in future to tell his critics to go to hell.

It is infinitely less damaging for the heir to the throne to travel in the style, comfort and privacy which his position warrants than to look like a businessman fudging his expense account.

1 February 1981

One picture from my TV screen last week is going to stay in my mind a long time.

It was that of a bright-eyed, rosy-cheeked nine-year-old boy called Eric who has spent the past 6 years in the care of the Greenwich Council.

In these 6 years he has seen neither his mother nor his father who, when they divorced, apparently didn't give a toss what happened to him.

He was pleading for a Mum and Dad whom he could love and whom he didn't have to share, except with other sisters and brothers.

I would like to think that the poor little mite will get his wish.

I would also like to think that the Mum and Dad who deserted him spend the rest of their worthless lives in hell.

1 February 1981

Sir Peter Parker, Chairman of British Rail, has sent out an appeal to leading British industrialists asking for help to save the rhinoceros which, according to Sir Peter, is rapidly nearing total extinction in the wild.

I applaud the effort he makes on behalf of poor, dumb beasts. And I ask only one thing.

Once he has saved the rhino, might he turn his attention to saving from extinction the poor, dumb beasts on British

Rail's 8.50 a.m. commuter train from Dorking to Waterloo?

30 December 1979

The words that twenty-three-year-old Flying Officer Vivian Rosewarne wrote to his mother just days before he and his crew and his Wellington were blown out of the sky over Dunkirk ring as fresh and clear today as they did those 40 years ago.

'You must not grieve for me . . . I have no fear of death. I am prepared to die with just one regret and one only – that I could not devote myself to making your declining years more happy by being with you.'

Does it make you feel proud that, after years of battling with the Ministry of Pensions, that widowed mother was awarded a pension of just £40 a year – and that when she died penniless and forgotten and alone at the age of ninety-one only charity saved her from a pauper's grave?

Yet, I suppose in a way Mrs Rosewarne died richer by far than the index-linked bureaucrats who treated her so meanly. For can there be greater wealth than the knowledge that once upon a time you had a son who so dearly loved you?

15 February 1981

••━••

On his way to holiday in Lanzarote last 13 November, Mr Frank Lancaster of Chobham in Surrey, bought a bottle of perfume in the duty-free shop at Gatwick Airport. It cost him £12.

On boarding the aircraft he discovered the same bottle of perfume was available for £7.50.

On his return, Mr Lancaster wrote to Allders International Limited who run the duty-free shop at Gatwick and asked them why there should have been such a difference in the price.

They replied that all prices in the duty-free shops 'are fixed by the British Airports Authority' and that they were passing on his complaint to that Authority who would be in touch with him.

From that moment Mr Lancaster heard not a dicky-bird until last week he wrote to me and I in turn telephoned the Authority.

Within twenty-four hours Gatwick were on the phone to him airily telling him that if he cared to return the perfume they would refund his money.

Did they really expect that he would be clutching the same bottle of perfume four months later?

More and more I become convinced that airport duty-free shops are among the most unpleasant over-priced rackets of our times.

15 March 1981

••━••

There are upright citizens who blow a gasket every time the magazine *Private Eye* is mentioned.

I know how they feel.

Yet but for *Private Eye*, which has just celebrated its 500th edition, Mr John Poulson would most probably at this moment be sitting in the House of Lords and that po-faced poof, Anthony Blunt, would most certainly still be taking tea with the Queen.

Surely, and if only for exposing those two creeps, *Private Eye*'s editor Mr Richard Ingrams will one day end up, a seraphic smile on his face, playing his organ in Heaven.

Wouldn't it be nice to think that his old chum Sir James Goldsmith will be demoniacally strumming the big bass beside him?

15 February 1981

Last Sunday morning, I went to the first tee in the final round of The Gambian Open the overnight leader in the amateur section three strokes ahead of the rest of the field, with a net 64.

I had visions of returning home with a cup.

Alas, it was not to be. The worst possible kind of disaster struck. I began to play my normal game. Five hours later, I staggered off the eighteenth green with just one remaining ambition. To get to the beer tent.

But I loved my 8 days among these warm, friendly people.

The only snag is that there are so many Scots working in The Gambia that if you close your eyes you almost feel you are back in Auchtermuchty.

The good news is that when you open them again and see the glamorous topless lassies by the hotel swimming pools, you know for sure that you are not.

15 February 1981

Six months ago I was interviewed on a Grampian TV programme by a blue-eyed lassie called Selina Scott.

I wrote at the time: 'She made Angela Rippon and Anna Ford look like a couple of sock-knitting crones. Is there a TV boss reading? Why should the whole country be denied a sight which the people in Grampian Region enjoy almost every evening?'

There was indeed a TV boss reading. And, from May, Miss Scott will be taking the place of Anna Ford on ITN.

I rejoice for her.

But isn't it a wry reflection on our TV orientated society that she will not only get £25,000 a year for reading out the news but will pick up a fortune for personal appearances and will most probably, in two or three years' time, be able to command £60,000 for her memoirs?

There are times when I wouldn't mind being discovered myself.

22 February 1981

I can understand why the pictures of naked beauty queen Gina Keer 'shocked and deeply upset seventy-year-old Mr Ken Bailey, organiser of the Miss Bournemouth contest. I can also understand why he scurried round to the Mayor's parlour to examine the evidence more closely.

It was saucy of Miss Keer to have posed nude for *Men Only* and even saucier for the magazine to have quoted her as saying: 'My boyfriend says I am like a tiger, once I get going . . . Sometimes I don't remember myself what has happened when we make love.'

But aren't the people who seek to depose Miss Keer as Miss Bournemouth taking the affair too seriously?

As far as her forgetfulness in passion is concerned, are there no respectable, married, middle-aged Bournemouth ladies willing to admit that exactly the same thing as happened to Miss Keer has happened to them? Even if with them, it has only been because they fell asleep in the middle?

8 March 1981

⸺

Yet another toddler has been savaged to death by Alsatians.

The dogs, of course, have been put down. They always are. When it is too late to bring the child back to life.

Wouldn't it be a better idea to put down the people who persist in keeping such dogs?

7 June 1981

⸺

The apology given by British Caledonian Airways to the anonymous vicar who, when his DC-10 was delayed by a mechanical fault, was given overnight accommodation in a Hong Kong brothel, could not be more complete or more contrite.

They explain that the incident would never have happened had the fault not coincided with a Chinese festival which meant that all the airline's normal hotels were full.

Just one thing puzzles me.

None of the lassies at the reception desk so much as flickered a slit-eye at the vicar.

It is true that his bed was circular in shape. But that might have been a quirk of modern fashion.

It is also true that the walls were lined with mirrors. But might not that have been to help him with his shaving?

How then, since presumably he had no previous experience, did he know he was in a brothel?

Is it just possible that, having placed his long-johns over a chair and his dentures in a tooth mug, the reverend gentleman made the fundamental mistake of ringing room service for a hot water bottle?

14 June 1981

*Last Sunday afternoon I saw a brown and white spaniel jump into the sea from a jetty at Cowes on the Isle of Wight.

At first I thought it was simply trying to retrieve a stick or a ball. But it quickly became evident that the dog had another purpose. It struck out in the direction of the mainland.

A cross-Solent ferry was entering Cowes. It missed the dog by feet. The dog still kept swimming.

I slipped my mooring and went in pursuit. A dinghy tried in vain to catch the dog and a Royal Yacht Squadron launch came out from the shore.

The dog was by that time almost all in. When it was brought ashore, it staggered for about ten minutes exhausted and full of water.

Why should it have acted as it did? It transpired that the spaniel owner's main home was in Shoreham, that he was about to go abroad on holiday and the dog was to be placed in kennels on the Isle of Wight.

Did the spaniel decide that he did not like the idea of kennels? Was he making a frantic effort to reach his own home?

For Shoreham some 46 miles away was exactly where he was pointing.

I do not know.

But I sometimes think that we humans, who regard ourselves as masters of the world, are not alone among God's creatures in having feelings.

21 June 1981

171

The Reverend Roy Bradbury of Calow in Derbyshire says that he is not going to marry any more drunks in his church. He tells of one bridegroom who was so stoned that he could hardly stand up.

I don't blame the vicar for being annoyed.

But what is to be done about the poor devil who would never go through with it at all if, stone cold sober, he had to look into the face of his bride and say, 'I do.'?

If booze is to be banned, might not the occasional blindfold be permitted?

12 July 1981

No one who heard the last speech of Lord Beaverbrook will ever forget it.

He was within days of death, and knew it. It was agony for him to walk even a few steps. Those closest to him did not believe that he could possibly attend the London dinner given to honour his 85th birthday.

But he did. And not in the wheelchair, which for weeks

had been, in the privacy of his home, his only means of transport. He walked in, back ramrod straight. He delivered a speech in which there was not one whimper of self pity. It was by far the bravest and the most brilliant speech I have ever heard.

They were the last words of a man who, by his exertions during the Battle of Britain, did so much to save our freedom.

Now Mr Malcolm Muggeridge, whose own contribution to our society could be comfortably accommodated in a thimble, and sounding as always as if he had two plums in his mouth, sneers on TV: 'I feel sure he was a bad man, someone who sold his soul to the devil.'

Was he? And if there is an after-life, is he now in Hell? If so, I have one last wish for him. I hope he will at least be saved the ultimate torture of being joined there by that unctuous old hypocrite Mr Malcolm Muggeridge.

5 July 1981

Sad, isn't it, the news from County Sligo where a 7-week pay strike by artificial inseminators has forced farmers to return to the old-fashioned way of covering cows?

The result so far is two bulls dead, and others buckling at the knees from the ordeal of performing more than a hundred times a week.

Still, there is a bright side to it too.

Isn't it a better way to go than ending up in a tin of corned beef?

28 June 1981

He was my room-mate and chum.

His name was Terry Cooper. He was just twenty-one. He had come to this country to help defend the homeland of his forebears.

One rain-swept morning he took off from a Fleet Air Arm base in Scotland.

He did not come back. Ever.

I wrote a faltering letter to his widowed mother in New Zealand whose only son he was.

Throughout the years she sent me Christmas cards.

Then she died. But ever since, other members of the Cooper family have kept in contact. Last week I lunched with a niece, who was not even born until 16 years after her uncle had given his life for Britain.

Yet here she was in London – a picture album proudly under her arm, pictures showing her uncle as he was all those long years ago.

I tell this story because there are times when I feel there are many people in this country who just do not understand the ties which bind the people of countries like New Zealand to this, their homeland.

I find it sad that when they come to visit us here, they should now have to enter through the door reserved for aliens.

5 July 1981

••◄••

In my mind's eye I can see the scene in the ballroom of Ryde's Solent Court Hotel.

The orchestra is playing the last waltz. In his arms debonair seventy-three-year-old Mr Philip Webb is holding sixty-nine-year-old widow Mrs Joan Tanner.

And there gnashing his teeth at the bar is Mrs Tanner's former regular ballroom dancing partner, seventy-one-year-old ex-Army captain Mr Norman Denman who has been dropped by Mrs Tanner for Mr Webb.

It is terrible that in his jealousy Mr Denman should have punctured the radiator of his rival's car, put water in the petrol tank and cut his brake hose. It is monstrous that Mr Webb should have had to walk his dancing partner home and then trudge all the 3 miles on foot back to Ryde.

But isn't there also a brighter side to the story? Isn't it going to boost the ego of every great-grandmother in the land?

At many a pensioners' social evening, can't you henceforth hear the glad cry go out:

Anyone care to tango?

21 June 1981